Grief Has No Rules

Holding Loss and Finding Light in Our Own Way

Copyright © 2025 by Cassie Swift et al

All rights reserved.

No portion of this book may be reproduced in any form without written permission from the publisher or author, except as permitted by U.K. copyright law.

This publication is designed to provide accurate and authoritative information in regard to the subject matter covered. It is sold with the understanding that neither the author nor the publisher is engaged in rendering legal, investment, accounting or other professional services. While the publisher and author have used their best efforts in preparing this book, they make no representations or warranties with respect to the accuracy or completeness of the contents of this book and specifically disclaim any implied warranties of merchantability or fitness for a particular purpose. No warranty may be created or extended by sales representatives or written sales materials. The advice and strategies contained herein may not be suitable for your situation. You should consult with a professional when appropriate. Neither the publisher nor the author shall be liable for any loss of profit or any other commercial damages, including but not limited to special, incidental, consequential, personal, or other damages.

ISBN number for this book: 978-1-7396179-4-3

Cover design by Heather Hulbert, www.heatherhulbert.co.uk

Disclaimer

Please be aware that this book contains topics of a sensitive nature, some of which people may find upsetting or triggering. For permissions, contact cassie@childrensmentalhealthmatters.co.uk

This book is not intended to be a comprehensive medical guide. The opinions and information expressed in this publication are those of the authors only, and they are sharing their expertise but do not represent professional advice. This book is not intended as a substitute for seeking professional medical advice, and the reader should regularly consult a medical expert in matters relating to their health, particularly with respect to any symptoms that might require a diagnosis or medical attention. The authors take no responsibility for any actions taken as a result of reading this book and do not assume and hereby disclaim any liability for any losses occurring as a result.

Trigger warning: please be advised that this book talks about issues which may be triggering, including death, ill health, child loss, suicide, eating disorders, mental health, and gambling.

Contents

1. Introduction ... 1
2. One Soul Broken into Two Pieces ... 7
   By Cassie Swift
3. Chronic Illness – Grief That Hides in Plain Sight ... 19
   By Sarah Burnett
4. The Power of Forgiveness ... 35
   and the Dilemma of Distance By Duncan Casburn
5. I Wasn't Expecting That! ... 45
   By Rachel Gotobed
6. Missing Pieces ... 57
   By Lou Hynes
7. Uncle Brian ... 71
   – My Father Figure and Best Friend By Emily Nuttall
8. Who am I? ... 85
   My Journey to Soft Nursing By Ashleigh Quick
9. The Silence That Follows ... 97
   By Kari Roberts
10. How to Grieve a Guy in Three Ways ... 107
    (Not A Romantic Comedy) By Emma Sails

11. Grace in Grief　　121
Grace, Growth, Glory – How to Manage the Unmanageable with Hope, Love and a Bit of Joy By Rebecca Williams Dinsdale

Other Collaborative Projects　　137
By Cassie Swift

Introduction

My intention when deciding to create this book about grief was to share my mum's journey with dementia. Sadly, we lost her last year, and I very quickly discovered that it was far too soon to go into this, so I pivoted my focus for my personal chapter.

Another reason I wanted to create this book was to give a different viewpoint from that of society. You see, there seems to be an idea out there that people only grieve when someone dies – but this is not true. There is also this misconception that people pass through five stages of grief, in a nice flowing process – also not true. And that some grief is in some way worse than others – for example, 'it was just a pet'. Ever heard that? Again, needless to say it's untrue. Finally, there is this idea that after a certain period of time, one should 'be over it' or 'have moved on'. Again, 100% NOT TRUE.

I am sure that if you have experienced grief of any kind, you will totally agree. And I hope in some way these chapters may bring you some comfort and reassurance that there is no set way to grieve.

I want to briefly unpack each of these, just to give a little more context and understanding to grief as a whole.

Let's start with what grief actually is. The Grief Recovery Method says:

"Grief is the conflicting feelings caused by the end of or change in a familiar pattern of behaviour." And it states that there are over forty different losses in life.

Notice that it says the 'end or change in a familiar pattern'; it doesn't just say the death of someone. Based on this, it is likely that everyone has experienced grief and bereavement at some point during their life. I want to add here that I am not a medical professional, nor am I a 'grief specialist', although I have trained in the Grief Recovery Method's 'Helping Children with Loss' course. I am simply an ordinary person who has experienced grief, researched lots about it, and am now here sharing it with you.

Whilst grief can, of course, be due to the death of someone, it can also be due to the loss of a pet, a divorce or relationship breakdown, the loss of a career or job, health issues and illness, grieving what could have been, parenting a child with a disability or SEN and again grieving the idea we had about being parent, moving house or area, even the loss of a sentimental item such as a soft toy or piece of jewellery. These are all vastly different, but each causes grief and bereavement in a way that not everyone may understand.

This brings me on to this idea that grief is dealt with in five neatly packaged stages – denial, anger, bargaining, depression, and acceptance. This was first described by Elisabeth Kübler-Ross in 1969 in her book, *On Death and Dying*. However, when Elisabeth first spoke about these stages, it was actually used to describe people with a terminal illness or diagnosis facing their own death – that of anticipatory grief. Over time, this seems to have lost its origins, and much of society seems to think this is how all people should deal with all variations of grief. But anyone who has experienced grief will know that it is a bundle of fluctuating emotions which varies on many different factors.

Then we have how people tend to 'compare' grief and loss – for example, that losing a pet isn't possibly as bad as losing a person (this is not my belief, I hasten to add here) – or question how it is possible to grieve a job loss when you can 'simply get another one'.

Anyone experiencing grief will do so at 100%. This means that it does not matter about all the details of who, what, where, when, and how. Rather, for that particular individual at that time, overwhelming surge of grief loss and bereavement will be felt as intensely, regardless. And that is why it is so important not to compare grief. It simply cannot be done. Everyone's grief is valid and doesn't need to be compared or justified, but instead it should be accepted and acknowledged with grace and compassion for what it is and with respect for the one experiencing it.

As grieving expert and author David Kessler explains, "Each person's grief is as unique as their fingerprint. But what everyone has in common is that no matter how they grieve, they share a need for their grief to be witnessed. That doesn't mean needing someone to try to lessen it or reframe it for them."

The last point I want to mention when it comes to grief is time. I find that time loses all meaning in grief, but that might just be me. There is, however, this idea that after a certain period of time, we should be 'over it' or have 'moved on'. I may be wrong here, but personally I believe you will never truly be 'over it' in the case of a death, as the person who has passed has a piece of your heart in some way, meaning you will always be reminded of what is no longer there. It's the same with ill health or parenting in ways we hadn't imagined, and whilst we would never change this, acknowledging the feeling of what could have been may still remain.

I do believe, however, that over time the intensity of the pain may subside, and I have seen a couple of analogies which really helped me.

The first is the concept of 'growing around grief' by Dr Lois Tonkin:

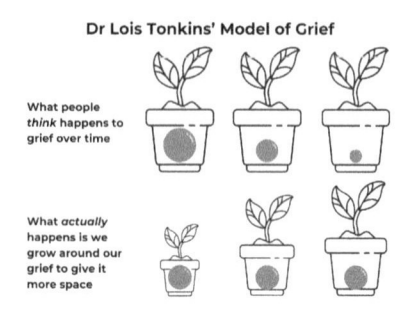

Dr Lois Tonkins' Model of Grief

What people *think* happens to grief over time

What *actually* happens is we grow around our grief to give it more space

As you can see, rather than the grief (illustrated by the ball) decreasing, what actually happens is we grow *around* the grief, accepting the things we cannot change, and growing to make room and allow in some 'normality', and even happiness, over time.

And secondly, Lauren Herschel shares the idea of a 'ball in a box' which she learnt from her doctor, as illustrated here:

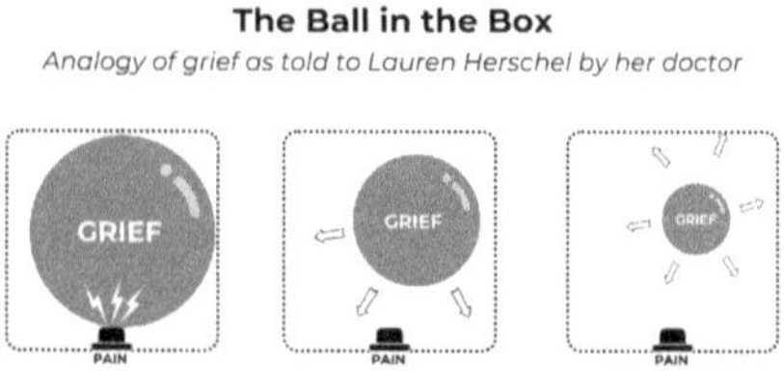

The Ball in the Box
Analogy of grief as told to Lauren Herschel by her doctor

This shows that initially after a grief event, the ball is so large that when it moves at all it relentlessly hits the 'pain button', causing the intense feelings of pain, hurt, loss, sadness, and hopelessness. In this concept, over time the ball does get smaller and can move around without always hitting the 'pain button'. But sometimes something may happen – an anniversary, a song, or even a smell – which will cause the ball to hit the pain button, and we experience the pain again. It just might be less frequent than before, and that is ok. As I said, I believe it will always remain, but it is how we navigate it that changes. I think of it as a combination of these two illustrations, which helps me on those difficult days.

My point here is to have compassion for yourself during this process, know that your feelings and emotions are valid, and that you are grieving in a way that is right for you. Of course, reach out for help and support from charities and organisations in your area. There are no rules, no timelines, and no shoulds when it comes to grief and grieving.

We see you and we hear you! We send you much love and healing as you walk this journey. You are not alone, and we hope that sharing our stories and experiences with you will provide comfort in knowing that we all grieve in our own way and for different reasons. We want you to know that you will find hope again, that you will find light in the darkness and grace in your grief. A grace that will allow you to hold the weight of the grief and still find a way to move, love, and speak again!

One Soul Broken into Two Pieces

By Cassie Swift

*"Things not what they used to be, Missing one inside of me.
Deathly lost, this can't be real, Cannot stand this hell I feel.
Emptiness is filling me, To the point of agony."*
– James Hetfield, Metallica: "Fade to Black"

"They can't stabilise his blood pressure; it is too low." The words were whirling around, not really making sense. Then came the earth-shattering sentence, "There is nothing else they can do!"

In that moment, everything went into slow motion as I collapsed to the floor, sweat rolling from my forehead, my body trembling so violently that I felt like a volcano was erupting in my heart. Tears like jagged pieces of glass were falling from my eyes, feeling as though they were ripping my cheeks as they landed.

Then... nothing. Just a cold darkness; an emptiness that I had never felt before; a complete void.

I was helped to my feet – my legs like jelly, unable to support my weight – sat at table, and a brandy handed to me. I drank it robotically, the disgusting taste clinging to the side of my mouth and burning as it made its way down my throat. I was certain I was going to throw up, but everything else had stopped, and a numbness entered my body. *Was it shock or the brandy?* Time paused, the business of the restaurant faded into the background, thoughts of it being my birthday left, and for what felt like an eternity this void of black, eerily silent nothingness remained.

"Cassie, Cassie! Look at me!" WHAM, it hit me again. It felt like a truck had slammed into me and I'd been thrown ten feet into the air. Then the noise returned louder than ever, feeling as though my eardrums were actually going to burst. *Was this actually happening? Had I zoned out for a minute and had some weird horrific daydream? Where even was I?*

I looked at my mum, and she too had tears in her eyes. So, it was true. This really was happening! *But why? Why him? Why my fiancé? Why us? Why now? He's only 30 years old, it's not fair! It's not right!* All these thoughts, memories of us, were whizzing through my head like a speed train on course to crash. It couldn't be true, it just couldn't. We had plans, we had dreams, our future was just coming together!

The rest of my 25th birthday passed, but I don't remember how. I do remember playing Metallica full blast in the hope that Dave could hear and would pull through. And there were moments of indescribable sobbing mixed with complete numbness, waiting for news, any news, about what was happening, praying the doctors would, by some miracle, help save the love of my life.

A glimpse of hope appeared when I received a call saying a new medication they had tried had raised his blood pressure slightly. *So, maybe things were going to be ok?*

As Dave lived in Devon and I in London, I spent hours tirelessly trying to find someone to drive me down, but to no avail. So, very early on Friday, 21st September, my mum and I set off to Paddington Station to get a train to Devon, continually praying Dave would pull through, praying I would get there in time and be with him.

At 9.30am, whilst at Paddington, my phone rang; it was the hospital. I froze, staring blankly at the screen, not wanting to answer, desperately praying for good news. I tentatively answered and lifted the phone to my ear, my hands shaking, my breath shallow.

"Is this Cassie Swift?" came the male voice at the end of the phone.

"Yes," came an inaudible squeak through a constricted throat. *Please no, please no, please don't say it*, were the words whirling in my head. Red hot tears filled and stung my eyes. I could sense in my gut what words were about to come out of this doctor's mouth, but I was willing with every fibre of my being for him to prove me wrong.

"I am so sorry, we did everything we could, but Dave die—" The phone fell from my hand, crashing to the floor, me following it and landing in a shaking, sobbing heap in the middle of the station.

I honestly cannot tell you what happened next. I remember my mum rushing forward and people running over, but it was though I was watching it; I wasn't there. My whole world had just collapsed around me, and I was left watching, in a place I did not recognise, not feeling anything in that moment other than that a part of me had just died, too, and was leaving me to be with him.

Let's go back to the start...

I had been through some very difficult mental health issues in my late teens and early twenties, winding up in various hospitals and feeling as though I would never have a future or be happy. As a result of this,

I went to stay with family in Devon, which is where I originally met Dave – the first time being in a cheesy nightclub (you know the type, way back in the early 2000s, right?). We got chatting and struck up a friendship.

I moved back to London to try and start putting together the broken pieces of my life and to look for hope where there had seemed to be none. Dave and I continued to message, which then developed into calls that lasted most of the day (and night), back when mobiles were pay-as-you-go.

As we grew closer, I decided to travel back to visit him, which in itself was a huge milestone as my crippling anxiety meant going out was a challenge, let alone travelling to Devon. However, I had a feeling it would be worth it and the rest, as they say, is history. For the first time I felt what it was like to be in love – to be fully accepted just for being me – cliché, I know, but also true! We had such a deep connection, one I cannot find the words to describe, but I knew he was my soul mate. (If you like *Friends*, he was my lobster.) We were two separate beings, but when we were together, we became one, entwined on a deep soul level. I knew we were going to be together forever. He was the one!

Dave was kind and loving, and his sense of humour was out of this world. Even on a bad day he managed to put a smile on my face. He loved Metallica and would endlessly talk about how amazing Kirk Hammett's riffs were in the song "Master of Puppets". We'd watch and listen to "Fade to Black" countless times, as he marvelled at the skill exhibited by this band. I learnt and found a new love and respect for music I had never heard before, due to the joy it brought him and the look on his face in awe at their skill.

Of course, not everything was perfect all the time, and having a long-distance relationship where neither of us could drive was hard work. But we were both invested and found it worth all the effort.

A couple of years into our relationship, we began planning for me to move down there; after all, Devon compared to London is a no-brainer, right? We wanted to spend our lives together, and for the first time in a long time I could see a future, with the person I loved. I felt like things were starting to change, as if the dark past that had consumed me for so long was finally lifting and there was hope – a light for the future. Things were going to be ok. I was going to get my happily ever after, after all.

Fast forward to Tuesday, 18th September, 2007...

Dave phoned to say he felt unwell and had gone to the hospital, where they had said he needed an emergency operation. He was in a great deal of pain but had made the nurse wheel him to a phone so he could talk to me. He apologised as he hadn't yet sent a birthday card (always last-minute was Dave). We both laughed, and I told him not to worry and that I would be down to see him after the operation. We ended the call, telling one another that we loved each other. Little did I know that would be the last time I would ever speak to him.

Thursday, 20th September, and Friday, 21st September (a tangled blur of time)

The operation, unfortunately, didn't go as planned.

I was out for a birthday meal with my family, and the plan was to head down to Devon after my birthday so that I could be with Dave after his operation. It was then that I received the phone call from Dave's mum and the horrendous events unfolded, culminating in me collapsing sobbing on the ground in Paddington Station. In true loving Dave style, I believe he held on long enough for my birthday to be over.

Eventually, I woke up on a train, but I don't remember how I got there. I awoke, having had an unimaginable nightmare that Dave had died. But when I looked across the carriage at my mum for reassurance that this was just a dream, the solemn look in her tearful eyes sent a chill down my spine.

"Is it true?" I whispered. "Has Dave really gone?"

"I am so sorry, darling. Yes." She could barely speak as she hugged me tightly.

Burning tears falling again, I must have cried myself to sleep for the remainder of the journey, and my mum only woke me up when we reached Devon. Usually, whenever I arrived there, Dave would be at the station to welcome me with a giant bear hug and a kiss.

But this time was different, and I felt like I had woken up in a parallel universe. The harsh reality that both he and our future had gone slapped me across the face with a reverberating sting, nudging me with a sharpened blade wherever I turned. The place I loved to be, what had been my happy place, had now turned dark. There was no light, just heavy dark shadows in every direction I turned.

It wasn't until I saw him that the reality fully encompassed me. When I gave him a gentle kiss on his head, I believe he knew I was there. But my whole world was destroyed, and I was back at the bottom of the black hole I had become familiar with in years gone by, meeting once again like old friends, all light extinguished. My knight in shining armour who had given me such hope for the future was gone, and I was left alone, empty, a shell, not knowing what I was going to do, and longing to be with him. Those destructive thoughts of ending my life returned once more.

The next week passed in a blur, shopping for funeral clothes. I had dissociated from everything, and the day of the funeral came and went. I remember all those details we all do – the overwhelming grief, the sense of loneliness, hearing stories shared from friends and family, maybe even laughing a little, then feeling a raging sense of guilt for daring to do so on such a day.

The thing with grief is it is like a wave, with moments of happiness and love, smiles on show, but interwoven with a heavy sense of loss. Accepting how we feel in each moment and learning to let it be ok is a hard thing to learn and harder to accept. But if there was no love and happiness, it wouldn't be followed by such immense sadness and loss.

I returned to London after the funeral, alone, scared, and spiralling deeper and deeper into depression. To ensure I was safe, I was made to stay with family, to keep an eye on me and make sure I didn't 'do something stupid'. I resorted to the most unhealthy and unhelpful coping strategies – drinking too much, smoking too much, buying things, and spending money I didn't have – all to try and fill this void. This monumental gargantuan hole was all-consuming, and I could see no point, no light, no hope. Everything that mattered had been taken from me, and I could see no way of ever moving past it.

So, what happened?

After a period of time – I don't remember how long – I wanted to return to my own space, as I thought it would help. With intervention from family and mental health teams, it was agreed I could go home, but I had people visiting three times a day to ensure I was ok. It wasn't an ideal situation, but it was worth it if it meant I could be at home.

Being there though, left me truly alone. Staying with family had ensured that there was always something going on. With children around, there is never any peace, yet now I was surrounded by the quiet I had so desperately yearned for, but I was paralysed with fear at the stillness and the never-ending expanse of time that would need filling. My cats rarely left my side and were one of the few things that kept me going.

Months went by in this self-destructive pattern. I thought people said time would make things better, but I now realise that time alone does nothing. Eventually, I realised that things couldn't continue as they were, so I reached out to have grief counselling. The waiting list was an extremely long one, but I waited in the hope that it would make everything better.

Eventually, I was allocated a counsellor. As this was before the time of online appointments, every week it would be a huge push for me to leave my house to go and see this lady. I cannot remember everything that was said, and I don't know if it really helped. But I guess the act of having to go out and talk about painful things must have been of some benefit.

Everyone was getting on with their daily lives, but for me every day felt like an uphill struggle, a battle. Nonetheless, I was getting through the days somehow, until I experienced another blow.

Dave had bought me a small elephant plushie that would go everywhere with me, and one day when I went to get it from my bag to put next to me, it had gone! So what? You might think it was just a soft toy, and I was 25 years old. That's true, but in that moment it felt like any progress I had made had just been unravelled in a millisecond. To me, it wasn't just a plushie; it was a comfort, bought especially for me, and it allowed me to feel closer to him in some way. It brought safety on the nights I would lay awake sobbing, unable to sleep, or when I woke up screaming because of a nightmare I'd had. And now it had gone.

As I mentioned in the introduction, grief isn't just caused by the death of a loved one. It can be caused by the loss of a precious gift, and that is what happened here. I had lost the one thing that allowed me to feel close to Dave, and that reopened the wound of the bigger loss. I still miss that plushie to this day.

The only thing you can do is to allow these things to come up and to have compassion for yourself. It doesn't matter what others may think or say; this is your journey. This was my journey, and the loss of this plushie sparked a wave of feelings and emotions which set me back. It was another painful reminder that what we have can be gone within the blink of an eye, and there is absolutely nothing we can do about it.

Slowly, after a long time of self-destructive behaviour and then therapy, I began to remember the happy times we had shared. Whilst there was still a pang of sadness that we would never experience that again, it was shared with a gratitude that we had enjoyed that time together.

The layers of grief still went deep. Things like the realisation I'd never get to walk down the aisle to meet him; I would never get to call myself his wife; we would never have a family together. But now I could remember the laughs we had, the moments we shared, the bond we had that was on such a deep energetic level, and which I believe is still there some 17 years later.

The sense of guilt sharing this story is also prevalent. My life slowly did move forward, and hope returned the day I found out I was pregnant. I am still single – a sign that I didn't 'work through my grief' in an appropriate way. But I have three beautiful children – something I once thought was never possible, that others don't always get to have, and something I never take for granted or would change.

The human brain is funny in the way it can yearn for something so much, while at the same time be beyond grateful for what you currently have. Undoubtedly, allowing the guilt to rise, acknowledging it, and then allowing it to pass helps immensely. But it takes time to learn this, and it's something that even now I struggle with at times.

I had never returned to Devon since 2007. The pain was too deep, the surroundings a reminder of what could have been.

But as I write this, it is 2025, and I decided to spend a weekend back in the very town where my future was to have been built – but this time with my children. The visit was a clear indication of how wildly different times are, a time in which it felt the two distinctively different worlds converged, and it was met with both joy and, of course, sadness. The joy that my children could see the place I have spoken about, where I once stayed, and the sadness of what could have been. Conflicting feelings of gratitude and guilt, growth and entrapment.

I took some time to go to the beach where Dave's ashes were scattered, for a moment of solace and stillness. As an overwhelming sense of his presence encapsulated me, something caught my eye amongst the pebbles on which I stood. Bending down, I lifted one particular stone and noticed its distinctive heart shape. My eyes filled with warm tears of love, as I realised that time and distance may pass, but there will always be a true connection with my one true love!

As I write and reflect on this, I am reliving everything as though it was yesterday. It's a sign that one never 'gets over it' or 'recovers' from the loss of a loved one, but rather that we learn to grow around the loss.

There is no easy answer or journey around grief; there are no simple steps to follow. It is a unique, often turbulent, rollercoaster of a ride. Dealing with grief isn't easy, and there are moments when your chest feels so heavy you do not know how you will breathe, but glimmers of light will begin to flicker again.

The ones who leave do not leave us completely. They had a piece of your heart, and whether it was a partner, a friend, a parent, or a pet, does not matter. There was a shared emotional, energetic bond with them, and although we can no longer see them, I believe they give us the strength we need to go on another day. Signs like a feather, a robin, a rainbow, or a song when we need to hear it, are all there to show us they are still nearby and that they reciprocate the love we still have for them.

Dave and I were one soul that has now been split into two pieces, but we still are and always will be connected.

There is always hope, there is always love, and there is a bond that can never be broken!

Dedication:

This chapter is dedicated, of course, to Mr Dave Stevens, the one who taught me what true love is, and for that I will be forever grateful. Until we meet again, my sweetheart.

Biography:

Cassie has been described by her children as "awesome, kind, incredible, caring, beautiful, and AMAZEBALLS". A single mother of three, her friends describe her as a kind-hearted, loving, and courageous woman who will stand up for her beliefs and the rights of others. Cassie experienced bullying throughout her entire school life and wishes she'd had someone to turn to, because her mental health deteriorated as a result. This is not something anyone would wish for a child, and no-one deserves to feel this way or experience what she went through.

Cassie has experienced a lot of grief during her life and wants to highlight to others that there is no one-size-fits-all approach when navigating grief.

She works as a Family Empowerment Guide, specifically with teens, to enable them to feel empowered about life. She helps them to manage big emotions in a positive way, accepting the true version of themselves. As a result, she brings calm and happiness not only to those she works with, but to the whole family. She is trained in several holistic approaches, including NLP, EFT, Hypnotherapy, and EFT specifically for teens, as well as a lot of life experience, which helps to put her unique spin on things.

Cassie is also a #1 Best Selling Author of nine books, four of which she co-created, as well as the founder and organiser of the Children's Mental Health Matters Summit. She has featured both on the radio and in six local newspapers, speaking about issues surrounding Children's Mental Health.

"Helping others, especially children, is my passion. I want to empower as many children as I possibly can!"

You can connect with Cassie here:

www.linktr.ee/CassieS

Chronic Illness – Grief That Hides in Plain Sight

By Sarah Burnett

"Grieving allows us to heal, to remember with love rather than pain. It is a sorting process. One by one, you let go of the things that are gone and you mourn for them. One by one, you take hold of the things that have become a part of who you are and build again."
– Rachael Naomi Remen

Unfathomable yet unrecognisable grief

I'm not sure I'll ever find words to fully describe the emotional pain of losing the ability to function overnight. Not being able to see or spend time with your young children for days on end, knowing that someone else is fulfilling your role and taking the toll as a result. You haven't died, but there are days when you wonder if you might as well have, and moments where it feels as though it would be preferable. You are missing from the morning routine, the school run, the dinner table, and the house in general. Getting to the bathroom and back is a victory hard won, and eventually, when you're well enough, you come to intimately know each step of your staircase. Can you imagine? Maybe you don't need to. For those at the very severe end of the scale of this illness, even that would be freedom of sorts. It's a very bizarre experience to witness those around you cope and move on without your input or presence.

Having had a couple of years of being mostly recovered from seventeen years of virally triggered ME/CFS, I knew when Covid came along what could potentially happen. In fact, what has unfolded in a large percentage of Long Covid cases over the last five years has come as no surprise whatsoever to many who were already familiar with this life-robbing illness. I wasn't consciously worried beyond a little niggle in the back of my mind. I had improved my immune system drastically with help from a brilliant nutritionist trained in functional medicine, had left post-exertional malaise, endometriosis, and much pain behind me, and I had successfully navigated some extremely stressful years as we discovered the reality of life, needing significant support for our youngest and all that that entails. Not only that, but I had returned to work part-time, teaching woodwind at a primary school – a personal comeback that unfortunately turned out to be very short-lived.

Context and nuance are key

A lot of the valuable advice we are given for dealing with grief I couldn't use until I was well enough to. As a person with Long Covid, severe ME/CFS, and dysautonomia, it really was a case initially of having to learn to lie there and exist with unbearable pain and find ways of mentally distancing myself for regular periods of time.

I was devastated and confused to discover that I couldn't lean into any of my usual strategies for dealing with this kind of hardship. I mean, I'd been here before to a certain degree, so I knew what to do... and yet I didn't. Because I couldn't. Instead, I had to just lie in bed, relent, and be – something that's incredibly hard to do when you have no control over your heart rate, temperature, multiple areas of intrusive pain, lack of balance, inability to tolerate sensory stimuli (even clothes hurt) – the list goes on. It was a living hell, for want of a better description, and I had next to nothing in terms of cellular energy.

Just a trip to the bathroom would metaphorically turn my limbs to lead and take hours to recover from. And all sorts, from hormonal changes, sensory factors, and feeling emotions, would trigger breathing difficulties, muscle pain, debilitating fatigue, and an inability to function for weeks and months at a time. I couldn't even listen to music and audio books; they were so draining. But ambient sounds helped, and watching the leaves dancing in the breeze on the trees outside when I had enough energy was good, too.

The infamous sodding virus

Covid for me was the weirdest but not the worst virus I've experienced. However, the aftermath was absolutely devastating. It took a few months to confirm, but overnight I had lost my ability to go for a walk, drink anything other than water or herbal tea, have a conversation with my children or husband for more than a few minutes in a day (sometimes not even that), the ability to do anything (including sitting up) without having to lie down and recover, and the energy to do things to distract me from the painful prison that was my body.

Physically and mentally, I had lost the ability to walk in a straight line, think coherently, form sentences (apart from the odd bit of writing), pronounce words correctly, tolerate light, sound, smell, touch, many foods and drink, exist without pain, sleep properly, and the assurance that people would understand (because many can't, even when they may want to).

On a wider scale, I lost the ability to see friends, attend flute group, cake group, Zumba, a parent-carer support group, occupational therapy and other appointments with our youngest, church, shopping, school runs, playing with and doing life with my family. I missed Christmases, significant birthdays, the few outings we manage as a family, and for the most part had to deal with it on my own, as life (challenging as it already was) had to carry on without me.

For a while I desperately held onto hope that I would recover enough that I could return to the school run at least, and also to the job that represented a return to work after taking time out to raise young children (having lost a previous job due to a milder but still life-impacting form of ME/CFS). But it wasn't to be. Receiving the letter to end that employment was heartbreaking, and yet I was so numb I could barely process it. I felt dismissed, tossed on the rubbish heap once again, and largely forgotten.

There were times where I wondered if I'd also lost my faith. Yet, despite dangling over the precipice a few times, I couldn't escape the knowledge that God was there as ever and holding me in all of this. There was much to learn, and His grace to me was providing a way out that could work with and around some of the trauma that I'd discovered in the process.

I was so used to well-intended but often misplaced advice, and somewhere along the line I had also lost the ability (certainly in this instance) to trust people, medical professionals, friends... even family. My brain had kicked into such a state of survival from the sheer amount of physical pain and symptoms that I was experiencing, that it took me months to shed a single tear and years to be able to feel and express emotion without a full physical onslaught and setback. Even joyous victory and the resulting euphoria would be followed by awful pain, crippling fatigue, and exacerbated symptoms. I never thought I'd be happy to feel sadness – such is the common desire for the more pleasant emotions – and yet I'm so grateful to be able to cry again and let the sad out when possible. It's necessary, and for the most part we're designed to do it.

There is no doubt that it is important to have a positive mindset when dealing with chronic illness, and yet the inclination from many people to offer advice such as 'think positive', 'be grateful', etc. without acknowledging and being prepared to sit in the hardship with us is something that can lead us to reject the reality of our experience, emotions, and ourselves. None of which is conducive to possible recovery or finding a way to accept and adapt to new circumstances.

From my personal bewildering experience, it can also be difficult to recognise or even express what we're feeling (internally), let alone find those who are able to truly offer what it is that we really need – a compassionate witness. Personally, due to a deep faith and belief in a loving God who chose to go through unfathomable pain and rejection as a human to defeat death through resurrection, I have never truly been without this (despite some periods of time where it felt that way). And yet, in terms of human beings – despite a few well intended offers of support from friends and family – I found myself in a position of needing a trained grief counsellor, and later a therapeutic coach who had recovered from ME/CFS themselves and was trained in helping people recover from fatigue-related illness. We may not be designed for isolation, but in this particular situation it needed to be trauma-informed support. And, due to the complex nature of my circumstances, I was very grateful for an online space and the financial resources needed to access this.

It's necessary to briefly address the hard reality that my journey over the last four-plus years has not involved grief on its own, and that trauma complicated things.

To quote David Kessler, "all trauma has grief, not all grief has trauma". My understanding from Dr Gabor Mate is that "trauma isn't what happens to us; it's what happens inside of us as a result of what happens to us". That's not to negate the severity of what may have happened to someone, but more to explain how it's possible to navigate the consequences and also to move towards, understanding the differing impacts the same event can have on two people. The similarity, I suppose, that makes it difficult at times to distinguish between Grief and Trauma is that there are complex emotions involved that need processing.

If there is trauma involved, then it is often the case that it can prevent us from accessing and processing the grief. There is a way through, but it's unique to the individual, and in the absence of a particular type of supernatural miracle, it needs appropriate and skilled support.

The gift of creativity, nature, and God's presence

Creativity has been and still is an incredibly powerful resource for processing the tough stuff. When I was well enough, I painted what I was feeling, wrote poems, took photos, journalled, prayed with words again, eventually sang again, and spent time in nature as much as was possible. I had also spent months lying on our daughter's basket swing, watching clouds. I embraced the parts of me that were hurting deeply and opened myself to the painful reality of our circumstances in small manageable amounts, so that I could gradually allow my body to heal and restore energy rather than continuously deplete it.

I rested in God's compassionate, loving, and peaceful presence and was grateful for songs and comforting words that would come to mind at the right moments. I saw hearts regularly, in clouds, oil, leaves, and all sorts of random places. I ranted, cried, prayed, and laughed in a WhatsApp group with a couple of friends. And eventually I walked and talked with a friend who lives nearby and hosted an online support group that came out of the hope programme for Long Covid. No-one had to explain themselves; we all just knew, because we were all living it in varying ways.

Eventually I trained as a therapeutic coach myself and continued to heal alongside others of all faiths and none, as we learned to help each other navigate our unique journeys. It's an absolute honour to be able to provide a safe space for someone to face their deepest hurt and guide them to a place of hope, trust, and curiosity again.

In one sense it's slightly easier to talk about this now, knowing that many of these losses have been or are in the process of being restored, but I do wonder if true healing isn't about the restoration. I wonder if it's in the acceptance and the surrender, relationship, learning to love ourselves, and learning to receive love, in all our pain and disappointment. Some things may never be restored. For example, I will never get back those years with my children, the days where I didn't see them at all, and others when I could only manage five minutes with them sitting on the bed next to me.

Noticing how much they had changed when I could finally do more than sit in bed with them would bring fresh waves of grief. It's wonderful to once again be able to do more than offer emotional support and presence, but there's no escaping that fact that they are both older now. There's a keen sense of the preciousness of time, and yet a natural graduation towards the inevitable letting go of our eldest and fresh challenges to face as our youngest develops and needs different support.

If you or a loved one are dealing with chronic illness, you may be questioning your experience and/or why you're experiencing it in the way that you are. Illness often brings with it myriad questions, confusion, bewilderment, frustration, guilt, shame, anger, and many other emotions, but one that is commonly misunderstood or overlooked is grief. I hope that through sharing some of my story you are able to find some hope and comfort, and that through acknowledging what is and working with what you've got, you are able to find or make more space for joy and contentment again where possible.

Having our daughter has taught me that a disabled life is a valuable life. I hadn't really had reason to consider it before, so it was confronting to discover my own ableism internalised and otherwise. A chronically ill life is valuable, too, and whilst recovery and healing are welcome and desirable, they don't make us more valuable or worthy of love, respect, and autonomy – even if that may be a common perception and one that we pertain to ourselves. All that said, it can be necessary to acknowledge and feel our loss in order to heal emotionally, even if that doesn't fully translate mentally and physically in the way we think it 'should'.

When grief comes into view

If grief is coping with the experience of loss, then anyone who has experienced significant and/or prolonged illness or disability will likely agree that it involves learning to cope with the experience of multiple losses, often the biggest being identity, confidence, self-esteem, self-worth and value, in addition to independence, autonomy, physical comfort, lifestyle, jobs, friends, community, sense of belonging, and more. It is a very strange thing to realise that you are grieving yourself when you are still here, but it's a thing – and a natural and necessary one at that.

Over the years I have grieved the little girl who loved to climb hills and mountains, who would run in big open spaces, and who had more energy than she knew what to do with. I suppose this might be a common and relatively unnoticed loss to many as we grow up, take on different things, and age. And yet I have also had cause to grieve the adult who had mostly overcome illness and was living a full and active life as a wife, mum, daughter, friend, and colleague, and was using a variety of gifts and talents to love and serve others.

It is incredibly hard to grieve after a significant and widely recognised loss, and yet we can be tempted to dismiss or miss entirely the challenges faced by those who experience subtler forms of loss. Often this type of covert grief is experienced unwittingly and in solitude, with little to no awareness or understanding of what's happening from the person or even those around them. They know something doesn't feel right, and in a society that is keen to dismiss difficult emotion and chase the pleasant ones – alongside labelling them as good and bad – they start to wonder if they're depressed or anxious. And whilst this might be the case, what they may be feeling are very valid and painfully difficult emotions in response to their circumstances. Which begs the question: how do we grieve when we don't realise that that's what it is? What even is it? I'd suggest that it's feeling and processing the complex layers of emotion in response to loss of what was, dreams that didn't materialise, and maybe never will. It's about honouring and letting go and, like layers of an onion, we may find we peel back one layer to discover more and more underneath.

Grief changes over time

Grief can change shape as we grow around it. Its intensity can change, too. This Long Covid grief now is cruising down the M6 feeling euphoric about a much longed-for trip to the seaside, a song coming on the radio, and a voice in the back happily saying "Silly Billies"! Momentarily laughing and then being consumed with an overwhelming sense of loss. Arms instinctively crossing over, hands reaching my shoulders in a comforting self-hug, tears silently falling, waiting for the wave to rise and settle. Why, you might ask? It doesn't have to make sense, it just is.

In this case, it was triggered by Olly Murs and a joy-filled memory of doing Joe Wicks sessions during the pandemic. We did it for our youngest mainly, but for me, conscious of my history with ME/CFS, I was also making sure I was as fit as I could possibly be. I mean, we couldn't afford for that to happen to me again, could we? Apparently, we could, and we have, although not without difficult consequences and an experience worse than I had imagined.

I felt joy for a moment, foolish for a split second, and then immense grief at the gargantuan pain and loss of the last four-plus years. I'm healing again, recovering bit by bit, and I can't deny that much positive has come out of this horrendous experience. And yet, I will never get those years back. I witness the effects of what happened playing out in various ways in my loved ones, and I feel intense emotional pain every now and then. And then it passes, making room for the now, reserving hope for the future – although not too far ahead, because we have a vulnerable child with learning disabilities.

I guess no-one can guarantee their children will have bright, shining futures, and all sorts can happen, but to have near certainty that they won't live independently and may need to rely on a government that doesn't value or understand their existence is another level. You just don't spend too much time there. I really do have to choose to let go, let God, and trust in things I don't understand, knowing that fear and anxiety in this instance is an understandable thing to be feeling but that it also doesn't need to be in charge.

Grief, although painful, isn't an enemy. It doesn't rise up, asking to be rejected; it asks to be seen, it asks to be acknowledged, it asks us to witness the difficulty, hardship, and loss, and respond with acceptance, love, and compassion. It doesn't need fixing; it needs allowing. And yet it doesn't stop there. It needs to be allowed to move through, as feelings pass and joy can return. In fact, joy and grief co-reside beautifully together should we allow them to. Eventually grief visits like an old friend (or an acquaintance, if friend is a step too far). We can say hi, thank you for showing me what matters to me the most, and thanks for reminding me that this loss matters.

I need to emphasise that chronic illness is not grief personified, and that there is far more to potential recovery than working with emotions. But, in more cases than we may realise, grief and trauma often have a part to play in preventing our bodies from accessing the state in which they can begin to heal. I know that I'm strong, resilient, and all the things that we often praise people with as positive. And with the right balance, they are really positive traits. The amount of people I come across who deal with chronic illness, disability, and challenging circumstances, who are relentless fighters, warriors, and persevere against all odds, is staggering. It adds insult to the way we are often viewed and the stigma we face. These are character traits to behold. And yet, when it comes to grief, the only way out is through, and the only way through requires surrender. The good news is that all those traits that can keep us stuck are the same ones that we can use to process the really tough stuff, and sometimes we need someone in the know to help us navigate this.

I can confidently share that there is life on the other side of this gargantuan experience. What has been lost may never be fully restored, and what is restored may not necessarily be what I wanted or expect. And yet, there is so much gained from learning the lessons it has taught, from growing, and from redirecting that love and pain to a greater purpose.

The importance of appropriate support

I've had all sorts of input from others over the years, some helpful and some not so much. But the things that have really helped me during this particular time have been the odd message with no need for a reply, someone sharing a pretty picture or something funny. People offering to meet up or catch up on the phone, even if it inevitably didn't happen because I wasn't well enough yet. The precious few who were prepared to wheel me about and sit in silence. Just non-pressured support, love, and appreciation, which didn't require anything in return really.

There is also so much power in a compassionate witness – one we can show all parts of ourselves to without fear or judgment or correction; one who can hold our pain with us and help us to distance from it when it becomes too much; one who can show us the way to do this for ourselves, so that we can either love ourselves (or as I like to view it, view myself in agreement with the one who created me and redeemed me and treat myself as such, too). I am so grateful to those who have been able to offer this, as well as many who have just listened, encouraged, and recognised the effort it's taken to exist and achieve anything like this. It's been essential in enabling me to find my way through.

Summary

There are no rules to grief, no neat stages, and other people can't go through it or navigate it for us. It's messy and painful, not linear, and something we have to do at our own pace. We need others who can offer compassion, comfort, and hope, without trying to solve it. We may need to learn to be able to embrace imperfection and raw authentic emotion in healthy ways. And we may have to find a way to own it, even though we haven't chosen it. Other people can't possibly know all there is to know about our unique situation, and often even we don't. It's worth going softly with ourselves and those around us when it's possible.

It's no wonder really that so many of us find it difficult. We've often been taught that there are good emotions and bad emotions, that we need to be fixed, that we need to be 'strong' all the time, that showing emotion is weak, that we must keep calm and carry on in all circumstances, that resilience is to keep going whatever the cost, rather than falling down and getting back up again.

In reality, and despite large opposition to the idea, feeling through the tough stuff is arguably one of the hardest and strongest things we'll ever do, being authentic with ourselves and emotions the same. And it's worth knowing that often those who shut us down do so because they feel uncomfortable with emotions themselves. It can be a common protective mechanism that comes from their own 'stuff'.

In short, grief can be an excruciating teacher that, should we accept it, can leave us with a considerable capacity for compassion and empathy for others. When we can learn to sit with really tough stuff, it enables us to sit with others in their tough stuff without the need to fix them or the situation for them. There is absolutely a place for deep suffering and beauty rising from the ashes, should we find ourselves able to accept it and allow it to. I hope you find your way, too.

Dedication:

To all my fellow humans dealing with disability, chronic health challenges, illness, and loss of any kind (and their carers, too). You are valuable just as you are, it's ok to acknowledge the grief, and it's also possible to reclaim joy in the tough stuff. You are unique, loved, not alone, and there is hope.

Biography:

Sarah Burnett, a former music teacher, is a faith-filled wife and mum of two children, both neurodivergent. One is in mainstream education, another who has higher support needs attends a broad-spectrum special school. Sarah has also dealt with various chronic conditions over her lifetime.

Her continuing recovery over the last four years from severe Long Covid has led to her retraining as a therapeutic coach, specialising in nervous system retraining. She has a deeper understanding of the challenges that her youngest faces and is grateful for the similarities her experience has allowed her to observe when the nervous system is stuck in a dysregulated state.

Parent caring when dealing with chronic illness is extremely challenging. Yet we do it, often with little support or true understanding of ourselves or our loved ones.

Creativity is a much-valued resource, and Sarah often spends time in nature with her camera. She also uses art, humour, music, and imagination to navigate the daily obstacle course that is being a parent carer.

If you would like support with the challenges that you are facing and to find a way to navigate them from a place of acceptance, understanding, and hope, please do reach out.

You can connect with Sarah here:

https://linktr.ee/SarahBurnettCoaching

The Power of Forgiveness
and the Dilemma of Distance By Duncan Casburn

"I'm not your son, you're not my father,
We're just two grown men saying goodbye.
No need to forgive, no need to forget.
I know your mistakes and you know mine.
– James Blunt, "Monsters"

NOTE: Before reading this chapter, go to YouTube and listen to James Blunt's "Monsters"

Before I go too deep into this chapter, I feel a brief history of my upbringing is probably needed.

To say that my father and I have had something of an up and down relationship would be an understatement. I come from a split family; only mine is slightly more split than most... Whilst my mother and brother lived in England, for most of my childhood I lived with my dad and his new family in Australia. He had been offered a 'too good to refuse' three-year contract in Sydney, and we moved there when I was ten. My brother had remained in the UK with my mum, knowing that we'd be returning after three years.

However, we never ended up returning, so we ended up with two very separate families.

Then, sixteen years ago, I met a wonderful woman and fell in love. And I wound up moving to the UK, as my wife is English.

What made this unusual childhood especially difficult was that I didn't, in any way, shape, or form, get on with my stepmother. There are many reasons for this, and to go into detail would take encyclopaedic volumes to cover – according to my therapist, at any rate.

On reflection, I can see my stepmother was battling many of her own inner demons. She clearly had many mental health issues clouding her mind, as well as wounds from her past. But she harboured a deep resentment towards me – I think subconsciously – and this led to a very fractured and tense relationship.

My dad has always been something of a hero to me; he's a very active member of his community and is involved with so many charities it's truly astonishing. He was even awarded the Adelaide Citizen of the Year Award a few years ago. He's been a successful businessman and just an all-round good egg.

What I've always particularly loved is his sense of humour. I used to listen to him at dinner parties, and he'd have everyone in stitches. I always wanted to have that ability. Last time he came to visit me in the UK, on a day out he made a comment to someone about my quick wit... and I think it was the best thing I've ever had anyone say about me. That it came from him made it mean that much more.

Sadly, the difficult relationship with my stepmother for many years left me estranged from my dad. I ended up moving out of home very young, as I could not deal with the constant abuse any longer. Over the following years, she made it increasingly difficult for me to see Dad, banning me from visiting the house and not being able to visit, even at Christmas.

The bigger issue for me was not that my stepmother was acting this way, but rather that Dad didn't seem to want to stand up for me. It seemed to me he was taking the path of least resistance, bowing to her demands rather than fighting to keep our relationship strong. I began to harbour a deep resentment that, as I saw it, he'd chosen an easy way out. Rather than standing up for me, he simply went along with things... so we grew further and further apart as time went on.

Shortly after I got married – a ceremony he sadly didn't attend – he and my stepmother broke up. Given the estrangement, I had no idea there had been any issues in their relationship, and I have to admit it came as quite a shock.

By now, of course, I was living in the UK, and the sheer distance made reconnecting difficult. But I truly wanted to repair our damaged relationship, and I could see that he did, too.

Over time, we managed to start the healing process proper. We talked over the phone, we shared deeply our feelings, and through the passage of time we came to understand a lot more about what we'd each been feeling. I think that we both came with a desire to own our own mistakes and seek forgiveness. That common goal spurred us on and allowed an honesty and integrity to the process. We both came to a new respect for each other and rekindled that father-and-son love.

A few years ago, he and his new wife (who, by the way, is AMAZING, and we get on really well) came to visit us in England. One afternoon, he and I went to my local and shared some drinks.

I had shared my first ever beer with Dad when I was sixteen... we'd been working hard in the garden together, and when we finished we sat together and shared that meaningful moment. It felt like a rite of passage into manhood. Dad told me that day that all he'd ever wanted was a relationship when he and I could enjoy a drink together.

So, that afternoon in my local pub, as we sat and had a drink once again, it felt like we'd come full circle. We didn't sit together just as father and son, but as friends and equals. It was the most special drink I've ever had. It felt to me that we'd truly left the past behind, and we had the rest of our lives to make better memories.

The key to this was – from both of us – the need to forgive. I remember hearing it said that harbouring unforgiveness is like drinking poison and hoping the other person gets sick. Holding onto all that pain and hurt was only causing more pain, and unnecessarily so.

Now, that's a long history condensed into a few paragraphs, and there's so much more to tell, but it's a good summary of our relationship, and it sets the scene for the rest of this chapter.

Over the last twenty odd years, my dad has been battling prostate cancer. He's beaten it every time, but it keeps coming back. Sadly, the last round of radiotherapy caused some bladder damage, so it was decided that a stoma would be needed. This was going to be done in the late part of 2024. But, before this could take place, seven months ago he went into hospital due to some bladder pain… and he hasn't left hospital since.

It's been touch and go for the last seven months, unsure if he'd survive. And what has happened seems to have triggered a form of dementia, and he seems very confused a lot of the time. I've been experiencing having to mourn him from a distance, preparing for the very real possibility that he may pass at any moment, and that the sharp mind and wit that were core to his being have, for the most part, gone. More than at any other time, I would love to be there for him right now and just hold his hand once more.

I recently contributed to another book with Cassie Swift, focused on Children's Mental Health. In that chapter I wrote about how this year has been especially challenging, as we've been facing mental health issues very deeply, and it's been one of the most difficult times in my life.

The challenges mean that I've had to be in full carer mode for this time, and I have to be available twenty-four-seven. This means I definitely can't leave to travel anywhere, let alone Australia. I can't go to see my dad, even if the worst were to happen and I had a funeral to attend.

It's ironic, isn't it? For years my father and I could be a million miles apart while sitting in the same room. Now we're joined deeply but separated by oceans.

A few weeks ago, I was flicking through YouTube music reaction videos. Music was something my dad introduced to me on my twelfth birthday, when he gave me a record player. Music is very much my shelter, and I often lose myself in its powerful healing. One song that popped up was "Monsters" by James Blunt.

I'll be very honest and say here that I don't particularly like his music; it just isn't my kind of thing (his voice is so high I think only dogs can hear some of it). But for some reason I clicked to listen, as I like him as a human being.

WOW!

It was one of those moments where everything I've been feeling is summed up in somebody else's words.

The song itself is basically a deathbed outpouring of emotion to Blunt's father. His father hasn't passed away, but the song is a statement of what his father means to him and how he truly loves him. But also, how the responsibilities and care that had once belonged to his dad were now his own.

The chorus in particular really hits home to me:
> *I'm not your son, you're not my father.*
> *We're just two grown men saying goodbye.*
> *No need to forgive, no need to forget.*
> *I know your mistakes and you know mine.*
> *And while you're sleeping, I'll try to make you proud.*
> *So, Daddy, won't you just close your eyes?*
> *Don't be afraid. It's my turn*
> *To chase the monsters away.*
> James Blunt, 'Monsters'

Those are some powerful lyrics!

The line that really grabbed me was this: "No need to forgive, no need to forget. I know your mistakes and you know mine."

When we face mortality, it can put into perspective what is really important in life. In my experience, the things left unsaid or undone are the weights that often bring us down the most. Unresolved conflicts and resentments can grow like noxious weeds in our minds and souls, poisoning the grieving process. I'm eternally grateful that my dad and I were able to repair past hurts, and that that weight is no longer something he or I have to carry.

In contrast, someone close to me had the opposite experience to mine here... we'll call her Jane.

Jane was adopted as a toddler to wonderful and loving parents. They are truly a blessing in her life – better parents than many biological parents I've seen. Jane's birth mother had left just as she was born. Her birth father tried to raise her for a year or so, but in the end couldn't manage, and he gave her up for adoption.

About fifteen years ago, Jane's birth mother reached out to try to reconnect. It turned out she was living in a psychiatric hospital, after being diagnosed with schizophrenia. The request to connect caused Jane a number of internal battles, as she had so many questions about why she'd been abandoned, and part of her coping strategy had been to somewhat demonise her birth mother. This is, I'm sure you'll agree, a very natural way to cope with these issues and move on.

After a lot of soul searching and internal conflict, in the end Jane opted not to reconnect, and the two never spoke. She simply didn't have the mental energy to deal with the powerful emotions – especially as she was dealing with her own mental health issues.

Then, six years ago, the sad news came that Jane's birth mother had passed away.

Jane talked with me about this at length. The realisation that so many questions remain – and will always remain – unanswered plays on her mind still. But the biggest thing that Jane told me lingers with her still is the fact that she never got to say she understands now why her birth mother left, and that she had been able to forgive her for this.

Her own battle with mental health had given her an insight into the struggles her birth mother must have been facing. It had allowed Jane to forgive, seeing the immense mental pressure that must have been on her birth mother. But sadly, it's something she never got to share; she never got to lift away that burden.

I got the chance to reconcile with my dad, and he knows that I love him deeply. And, in turn, I know he loves me. That is a burden I don't need to carry any longer, and neither does he.

All this has massively changed the way I see life now. I always try to keep any conflicts or differences in perspective. I would rather simply move on, not bearing any grudges to anyone, and hopefully they don't against me.

A few months ago, I had a disagreement with my neighbour, who's never particularly liked me for some reason. He'd overheard me making a comment about a fence he was building and took offence. He'd misunderstood my meaning, but he confronted me and said some pretty nasty things.

This played on my mind for days... I genuinely hate having any sort of beef with anyone these days. So, in the end I bought a six pack of beer and gave it to him, apologising for my comment about his fence, and said I just wanted to bury the hatchet. He, too, apologised.

He now makes a point to say 'Hi' whenever he sees me.

What feels best is that the action of sharing a drink echoes that one with my father.

Dedication:

For Dad: you gave me life, music, humour, and light. I will always endeavour to pass these gifts on.

Biography:

Duncan Casburn is a devoted father of a wonderful daughter with Autism and PDA (Pathological Demand Avoidance), embracing the highs and lows of neurodiverse parenting. He has a YouTube channel — PDA DAD UK — reflecting his life, a fusion of personal narratives, shared experiences, and informative content.

PDA Dad UK is a dedicated space for understanding Autism, Pathological Demand Avoidance, and the broader spectrum of neurodiversities, and the channel unravels not just the 'what' but the 'who' behind these conditions. While the terms Autism and PDA are commonly recognised, true understanding is often lacking, and that's where the channel comes in. Every video is a heart-to-heart conversation, a professional insight, or a beacon of enlightenment on the nuances of neurodiversity.

Beyond just sharing, Duncan holds roles that connect him deeper into this community, serving as a Carers' Ambassador for Devon Carers, an Ambassador Volunteer for DiAS (Devon Information Advice and Support), and an Ambassador for the PDA Society.

You can connect with Duncan here:

https://linktr.ee/PDADadUK

I Wasn't Expecting That!
By Rachel Gotobed

"Life is what happens to you while you're busy making other plans."
– Allen Saunders

"For I know the plans I have for you," declares the Lord, "plans to prosper you and not to harm you, plans to give you hope and a future."
– Jeremiah 29 v 11, The Bible (NIV)

The inclusion of my story in this book is not because anyone died, but rather because I find myself living with a sense of unexpected difference on my journey as a parent. I have two wonderful adult children who both bring unending joy to my life. However, I have had to come to terms with living this unexpected path, as my daughter is autistic and moderately learning disabled. Because I have gained so much more by living with this unexpected difference, I struggle to describe the emotion that accompanies living with this change in expectations as grief or loss, and yet there is a feeling that sometimes lives with me that is grief-like. This is in no way a reflection on who my daughter is, because there is nothing I would change about her, but rather it is because of what is not, nor ever will be, and living with this feeling is one that requires ongoing processing and continual loving acceptance.

Having struggled to conceive our son, I wasn't expecting to fall pregnant a second time so easily, if at all! However, when our daughter was born, a 5lbs 15½oz beautiful bundle of joy entered our world, we felt our family was complete. Although her walking was a little later than expected, nothing else about her development had worried us except for her speech, and this was identified at her two-year review. We were duly referred to speech therapy, who on their first encounter declared that she was just letting her very verbal brother speak on her behalf and that, because she was making appropriate sounds, there was nothing for us to worry about.

Taking her for weekly speech therapy sessions over the next few months, it was just after her third birthday that I took a big breath and voiced my concern out loud as to whether this speech delay could be something other than just that. And when the therapist was non-committal, I asked for a referral to see a paediatrician. Because of her overall well-being and ability in other areas, we were again met with uncertainty as to the possibility of anything other than speech delay. And as she was to start nursery school in September, it was agreed to see how that went and then reconvene.

Having previously taken our son to the same nursery, what happened after our daughter's first few mornings there was so unexpected. Greeted by the headteacher, he ushered me into an impromptu meeting where it was explained that our daughter needed extra support, and for the school to access additional funding I needed to agree for her to see the educational psychologist. The next few months saw a barrage of meetings, questions, and form-filling that felt very alien to us. And alongside repeat visits to the paediatrician, it was just over a year later that we found ourselves in a strange room with a multidisciplinary assessment taking place.

It was a cool, late September morning when I first heard the words, *"It is our considered opinion that your daughter is autistic,"* said aloud. As they were spoken, it was as if a gong was simultaneously struck in my head, and as it resonated, the pain was both physically and emotionally shattering. It wasn't that this diagnosis was completely unexpected. Even though I had avoided researching signs and symptoms, in my heart of hearts I knew this was the most likely outcome, but what I wasn't expecting was the darkness that engulfed me as the words were said.

Up until that point, there had always been hope. Hope that it was nothing really. Hope that she was just a little slower in her development and that she would eventually catch up. Hope that I was just a paranoid mother who needed to be more patient! Yet in that moment, hope felt all but extinguished, and the ground shifted in a way that brought an unexpected realisation that life had changed forever. The rest of the words spoken that morning – those offering support and encouragement by well-meaning professionals – were all muffled by that gong crashing through my mind. And it was only after we were gently escorted from the building that the reality of the words spoken hit me, and the tears that I had been fighting back began to silently flow. Why her? Why us? What now? It's not fair! As we made our way back to the car, these inner cries of anguish were heard by God alone.

This response was unexpected. I thought I had prepared myself for this outcome and that my faith was ready to face it. But how wrong was I? In an instant, likely and actually had proved poles apart, and my faith floundered as previously perceived acceptance drowned in despair. And as the wave of tears kept falling on our journey home, my mind filled by more unanswerable questions. How do we tell people? What do we tell them? How can we help them understand when we don't understand ourselves? What does this mean for today? What does it mean for tomorrow? However will we cope?

"Mummy." A little voice from the back of the car, now speaking more but still delayed, suddenly sounded above the reverberating gong in my head. And as I turned to look at her, she smiled – a smile so wonderful that immediately the darkness scattered as the light of her face momentarily stilled the turmoil of my mind. Here was the reason for my heartbreak. A little girl, happy, healthy, beautiful – for whom nothing had changed that morning! Her need of me was no greater now than it had been a few hours ago. I was the same "Mummy" and she was the same child. So, why was I crying?

I now know that having a child with additional needs is one of those life experiences that you can only fully understand if you live it. So, while people received the shared news sympathetically, it was beyond most of their comprehension to grasp exactly how momentous this diagnosis felt. I remember at the time trying to find an analogy to explain how I was feeling and suggesting it might be something like when you know a loved one has a terminal illness and, even though you are expecting them to die, when it happens it does nothing to diminish the actual loss felt. Now, having also lived that experience with my dad dying of pancreatic cancer a few years later, I know it felt very much like that. But it was more confusing, because I hadn't lost anyone yet knew the life I'd expected had now changed.

In the months following this, the sound of that gong became an unwelcome companion, especially when sat in endless medical appointments and education reviews. The focus of every conversation was very negative – what she couldn't do, what additional help would be needed, who was going to pay for it. Once a Statement of Special

Educational Needs was eventually formalised, there were some weeks when life felt a bit more manageable, although it was never too long before the gong sounded again!

Filling in forms, in which you must convey every worst-case scenario to even stand a chance of being awarded benefits, was a heart-wrenching, thankless task, but on the advice of another parent's experience, I found myself doing them in the middle of yet another night when our daughter didn't sleep. We lived in a constant state of exhaustion, so reading them back in the cool light of day, I was shocked at what I had written regarding the extent of her care needs. However, I sent them off with no real expectation of being awarded anything, because to me it was just what any loving parent would do for their child.

That said, I was then totally unprepared for how loudly that gong reverberated again when the letter arrived saying we were awarded the highest level of Disability Living Allowance payable for children. To me, it felt like such a huge, unexpected difference, because someone not known to us had now determined that our precious child needed much greater care than other children her age, and I hadn't foreseen that. While struggling with the enormity of this, I then had to face the excruciatingly painful reality that my role in full-time church ministry was untenable in the face of her care needs, and resigning from this brought what felt like grief upon grief, and a loss of self that took many years to restore.

Even living with all this unexpected change, we seemed to adapt as best we could, and life became more settled with our two young children. I thought I was doing pretty well at muffling that gong of difference until I arrived at school one morning and found the Special Educational Needs Co-ordinator (SENCO) unexpectedly waiting. Transitions and milestones in our daughter's education have been one of the areas of difference in expectation that have proved most pronounced, so as the SENCO spoke that morning, the gong began crashing loudly again. She kindly explained that education in this mainstream school may not be the right option for our daughter, and that we should consider looking at the possibility of a special school placement. Nothing so far had prepared me for how enormous even the suggestion of this felt, and for how loud and long that would keep the gong reverberating.

Thankfully, a peripatetic autism support teacher had recently been assigned to visit and assist the staff working with her, and we were aware that she headed up a small autism specialist unit within another mainstream school not too far away. Visiting there, we immediately felt this would be a perfect fit for our daughter, but we knew the places here were highly sought after and were informed there was only one space available for September. It was agreed that we would put her name forward and, having got all our praying friends on the case, we were delighted when the place was offered to her.

Leaving mainstream school and separating our children from being educated in the same place was hard for us all. Carefully planned transition visits helped prepare her for the change ahead. But even these had in no way readied me for the depth of feeling that came when having to put my precious child on an assisted transport bus and let someone else take her to school instead of me, before then taking my son back to the same school she no longer attended. The gong crashed so loudly that day that I thought it would never stop! Before too long, however, this new daily routine became more bearable, and as we began to see her thrive, we knew we had made the right decision even though it had been so tough to make.

Many of the expected indicators of an ordinary child's life have set that gong of different expectations ringing in the ensuing years.

To me, both of my children are extraordinary in their own way, but having an older child who excelled in education made us very aware of the danger of comparison and how we needed to celebrate the achievements of them both that weren't purely academic. That said, however hard you try to do this, it is difficult to avoid those feelings of unexpected differences to all children when yours is the one who isn't invited to parties, playdates, or sleepovers; who doesn't get a part in the school play or chosen for a sports team; nor get their exam results when their peers do. Of course, we loved celebrating some of these things with our son and sought to always find different things to celebrate with our daughter. But at the same time, I couldn't help but notice how different life sometimes was for her, and these expectations not happening resulted in many, mostly hidden, tears.

For our daughter, this unexpected route through special education has been brilliant, and it is now one that I will always recommend other parents to take if the opportunity arises. Even here, the apprehension of her annual Statement review, and then later her Education, Health, Care Plan review, always set that gong of difference off again. But as they were managed with such care by the teachers involved, I could usually muffle the sound and associated feelings relatively quickly, especially as they were always so keen to accentuate her achievements. The help and support received from these amazing specialist teachers and assistants meant our daughter flourished way beyond our expectations, first through primary school, and this then continued when we successfully secured her a place – again with much prayer surrounding it – at the only autism-specific secondary free school in the area.

Here, the curriculum was differentiated further to accentuate her strengths, and throughout her eight years there we witnessed her grow and develop in ways far beyond anything we ever expected. Their holistic approach to her education mattered far more to us than the qualifications she also achieved, but particularly their championing of her love of art meant she was guided into passing both her GCSE and A Level – of which we wouldn't be prouder if she'd got a PhD! Amidst challenging pandemic conditions, we then had to find a post-19 college place, with limited opportunities to visit any suitable options. Again, our prayers were answered, and we were blessed to be offered a place at the only specialist provision we were able to visit due to lockdowns, and she continues to thrive while attending there.

Somewhere amidst all of this, I found a way to better embrace the unexpectedness of this parenting journey, yet at the same time it has never stopped me from sometimes wondering how different life might have been. The loss of the freedom of other day-to-day life choices is very real, and sometimes I have longed to just be able to do what other families do. Instead, whatever we did, wherever we went, always had to be preceded by in-depth analysis of how our daughter might manage in any given situation, and we have needed to miss special events because we knew she just wouldn't cope. The same was true of family outings and holidays – which we recognise was often difficult on our son – and meant we were limited as to where we were able to go all together, or we were required to make the tough decision to split up as we tried to ensure both of our children felt loved and valued for who they were.

Each year in the days leading up to our daughter's birthday I have found that painful gong of unexpected difference resounding again through my mind, especially as I have had to face the reality gap between her increasing physical years and her younger loves and abilities. As she has got older – and particularly on milestone birthdays like 13, 16, 18, and 21 – that difference has become more prominent, as the gifts she wanted were very unlike most girls her age. Sometimes I now have conversations with young women who are the same age as her, or see friends doing things with their daughters that I would love to do. It is then that I feel a sting of longing to be able to talk to my daughter in the same way, and for us to be able to experience life in the way they do. And the fact that we can't hurts... a lot.

However, there have also been times when I have felt abundantly blessed in not having to deal with problems faced by other girls her age. Our daughter hasn't ever stressed over exam results or a future career; worried about her image or what people are saying about her on social media; dealt with the heartbreak of broken friendships or relationships; or had to deal with the many complex issues that face young people, and especially young women today. Instead, she is just about free from all of that, and lives in a happy, mostly carefree, routine-driven world of home, college, church, and "me" time, while letting us worry about the many different challenges life brings for her.

Sometimes that gong has gone off because of the words and actions of others. Strangers who point or laugh, or feel they have a right to comment on your child's behaviour and give unsolicited parenting advice. Harder still is when well-meaning friends say the most inappropriate thing, and you find yourself criticised for a choice made with your child's best interest at heart. Sadly, this has even been our experience within the church, and instead of always finding it to be a safe place, there have been times when I have considered never going back because of people's unkindness. Over the years we have been made to feel that our daughter's needs were a nuisance, an inconvenience, expendable for the good of others, and that we had no right to expect reasonable adjustments just for her benefit. By the grace of God, and for my own soul's wellbeing, I've had to learn to forgive many things said or done from what I hoped were places of fear or ignorance, and I've tried my best to respond in ways that have helped increase awareness, acceptance, and inclusion.

So, to date I've survived the resonance of that gong and found ways to adapt and thrive despite it. Many a crashing has been thwarted or side-stepped along the way, but at other times it's knocked me off my feet and taken a lot for me to get back up again. It's never too long before something triggers its sound, and I am now aware that decisions need making concerning our daughter's future, and that this feels like the biggest change in expectations of all.

Having supported our son through university and leaving home, once more I'm living unexpected differences that make my heart hurt. And my tears freely flow at the thought of never being the mother of the bride or holding my daughter's child. Worse than that, however, is the most painful thought of all, that there will be a time when I won't be around to look after my precious, still so vulnerable child. And as we begin to explore what this looks like, I find myself desperately wanting to put my head in the sand so I can't hear the gong, while at the same time needing to do everything in my power to ensure that she gets the opportunity to live her best life going forward.

Yet whatever my feelings are, and however often or loudly that gong resounds in my head, what I have learned over the years is that this is as nothing in comparison to what our daughter needs to overcome each day just to survive in this non-autism-accepting world. I cannot begin to understand how difficult it is to live when your disordered senses are impossible to control and you are constantly overwhelmed, or your anxiety levels are such that you'd rather sacrifice doing something you really love because it impacts the feeling of safety found in your routine. Neither do I know how it feels to want to be able to communicate your thoughts and emotions but not be able to find the words, or to experience a meltdown that brings physical pain and self-loathing but is the only way to let out the build-up of stress inside your head. All this, and undoubtedly much more besides, is what she bravely deals with every day just to cope, and her fortitude in doing that gives my clanging gong meaning, purpose, and perspective.

Our daughter loves to sing, and popular songs of strong female vocalists are always coming from her bedroom. But another of her favourite songs comes from an animated version of the Bible story of Esther, and these words she sings ring truth far above that gong of unexpected difference. "The battle is not ours, we look to God above, and he will guide me safely through and guard me with his love. I will not be afraid; I will not run and hide for there is nothing I can't face when God is by my side."

I may not have been expecting this different parenting journey, but I now know that hope was never lost, and that I am a far better person because I have needed to journey this way. I will be forever grateful for the many amazing people who I have only met because we travel this unexpected road, and for the fullness of life that is mine because our daughter is "au-some".

Dedication:

Adrian, Jacob, and Hannah – more love and joy shared than ever expected!

Biography:

Rachel Gotobed loves being with people and is energised by working with those who share her passions and interests. Her husband and two adult children are central to her world, along with her extended family, her friends, and her church family.

Rachel's Christian faith is integral to all she is and does, and this is reflected in her work within the Family Ministries Department of The Salvation Army across the United Kingdom and Ireland.

She especially loves baking cake, writing lyrics and scripts, going to the theatre, drinking coffee, and eating afternoon tea. She is a passionate advocate for autism acceptance and inclusion and has supported many families who share this different parenting experience.

Missing Pieces
By Lou Hynes

"It is not the critic who counts; not the man who points out how the strong man stumbles, or where the doer of deeds could have done them better. The credit belongs to the man who is actually in the arena, whose face is marred by dust and sweat and blood; who strives valiantly; who errs, who comes short again and again, because there is no effort without error and shortcoming; but who does actually strive to do the deeds; who knows great enthusiasms, the great devotions; who spends himself in a worthy cause; who at the best knows in the end the triumph of high achievement, and who at the worst, if he fails, at least fails while daring greatly, so that his place shall never be with those cold and timid souls who neither know victory nor defeat."

– Theodore Roosevelt

When the piece was whole

Everyone has a before and after in life. I have two. The first of them was what we fondly termed 'The Day Everything Changed'. It took place on June 28th, 2012. The other? I'll come to that later...

Pete and I had met at work; both new-starters and both, unbeknownst to us, in need of new starts. After I'd been to New York and Pete had been sent to the Shanghai office on business, we agreed to exchange notes on our respective trips when we were back. That evening, as friends and colleagues, we both shared everything that was in our hearts and minds. Everything. And there was a *lot* to share! It wasn't intentional. But there was an instant mutual trust, respect, and connection.

Later, as we shared a taxi (we'd drunk our way through more than one bottle of Pinot Grigio, and he insisted on seeing me home!), he took my hand. This innocent action took my breath away. A gesture of solidarity. That he cared. That he *saw me*.

From that moment on, everything changed. The world shifted on its axis a little, and there we were. Soulmates. There was nothing we could do to stop it, even if we'd wanted to.

On paper, you'd never have seen it coming. Pete was the opposite to me in so many ways. He, a scientist, loving precision and logic. Me, a linguist, loving people and feelings. But we were the perfect complement for each other. Him calming and grounding me when I needed it most. Me providing him with a spontaneity and fire he hadn't experienced before.

Pete was funny (hilarious, in fact), warm, kind, and clever.

I was going through a divorce when we got together, and he had an innate ability to know exactly what I needed, to say exactly what I needed to hear. He always managed to stop me from flinging retaliatory emails back to my ex-husband with steam coming out of my keyboard (well, most of the time, anyway!).

Pete called me his 'missing piece'; the counterpart to the parts he didn't have; the yin to his yang. He'd sign every birthday, Valentine, or anniversary card with this, even down to the notes he'd hide beneath the pillow or inside a notebook if he was ever away for a night. He even had cufflinks specially made for our wedding day. Jigsaw pieces. One with P&L. The other with 17/10/2017, our wedding date.

So, we weren't the same shape, these missing pieces who somehow found each other when we needed to find someone the most. But we fit together and completed each other's puzzles. Pete was delivered to me as my soulmate. My missing piece. And I his.

The moment everything changed (again)

The second of those before and after moments where life changes in an instant was Saturday, December 3rd, 2022.

We'd all had the usual autumn/winter cold; even the kids were snuffling and coughing. Pete had also been going through a really stressful time at work, having to make a significant number of his team redundant, and it had taken its toll on him emotionally.

Consequently, he was looking forward to a week off work. A week where we would go Christmas shopping, chill, spend some time together, and look forward to the magic of the holiday season.

When he complained of a headache and feeling rough, I reassured him that the week off was what he needed, to forget about all the upheaval at work and focus on himself. Now, let me tell you this, Pete was not your typical 'man flu' kind of guy. He rarely complained. He was one of life's non-complainers. God, do I wish he'd complained more.

After taking himself to bed early on the Friday afternoon, I'd run around like a headless chicken trying to navigate the Friday afternoon traffic jams, drop our son to football training, whizz my eldest — Pete's stepson — to his dad's, all while worrying that I'd left our daughter 'on her own' with her daddy poorly in bed. When I finally got back home after what felt like a fraught few hours and poured myself a glass of amaretto, Pete had got himself up. We watched the final episode of the Euro '96 trilogy we'd been watching, reminiscing about Gascoigne, Lineker, and the drama that played out.

Little did I know the drama that was about to unfold in our own lives.

Saturday morning arrived, and Pete was already up when I came downstairs. Sitting in his chair, Lemsip in hand, he was catching up on his beloved New York Islanders ice hockey highlights, as per usual.

It wasn't long before he told me, rubbing his hand behind his ear, "I'm going to go back to bed, Lou. I think I'm starting to get an ear infection." He got himself snuggled under the duvet, with me bringing him hot honey and lemon, and some porridge.

The kids and I settled in for a cosy day, too, with me going and checking in on a sleeping Pete every so often. Matilda, our daughter, aged six at the time, drew him a lovely 'Get well soon, Daddy' picture and put it on his bedside table. It was a drawing from his baby girl that he'd never get to see.

As the dark day turned into evening, the children and I had our dinner and snuggled in to watch a film. It was not the evening I'd had planned at all, as I was supposed to be putting my sequins on and going out on the town with my best friend for our annual 'Christmas Do'.

As the movie was starting, we heard the loudest thud from upstairs. We all looked at each other, and I got up to see where it might have come from. "Ooh!" I said brightly to the children. "Daddy might be up!" I went upstairs to see what might have caused the huge crashing sound we'd heard. I looked into each bedroom then went up to the loft conversion where our bedroom was. Nothing. No-one in bed. I couldn't find Pete anywhere.

Thinking nothing of it, but also thinking it really strange at the same time (where was Pete?), I decided to do another check of all the rooms in the house. The sound had been so loud, so unignorable, that I had to. And I couldn't find my husband.

Calling his name, I went back upstairs to our bedroom and looked where I hadn't looked in my first sweep of the house.

Lying unconscious, between the bed and the window on the floor of our bedroom, was my husband. I couldn't explain how he had got there. But I know for certain I wasn't supposed to see him there the first time I'd looked. I think the Universe had my back in not showing me how Pete had got there and what I might have seen had I spotted him on my initial look into our bedroom.

What happened next was a blur. 999 calls, panic, sirens. Paramedics pushing aside our bed and furniture like they were skittles, in a bid to get Pete out of there. Terror. Phone calls to my friend for her to come and sit with the kids so I could go with Pete. Hospital. Waiting in the corridor while Pete, my husband, my missing piece, was in resus. Being taken into a room by the consultant and vaguely thinking, *Oh, this isn't good if he's taking me into a private room.* Being told the next 24-48 hours were critical. Going in to see him. My parents arriving. Tears. Shock. Confusion. Tubes. Machines. Beeps. Intensive Care Unit.

When I finally left the hospital with my mum in the early hours of Sunday morning, so that I could be home when the children woke up, all I knew was that he was in a very serious condition. He had swelling on the brain and they didn't know the cause, but they were giving him all the drugs and care and doing everything they possibly could.

My husband was strong, healthy, and fit. He'd played sport of some kind all his life and had laughed when he turned 40 earlier that year, saying he wasn't going to let a 4 at the beginning of his age be an excuse to slide into 'Dadbod' territory.

Going in the following day, again the ICU consultant took me into the private room to deliver the news that overnight Pete had become less receptive, that the swelling on the brain was so severe it had gone to his brain stem, and that he was, to all intents and purposes, brain dead.

My super clever, witty, funny, full-of-life husband, who valued learning, knowledge, and his own amazing brain so much... oh, the irony was not lost on me.

Further tests the following day confirmed that Dr Peter Hynes, my amazing husband and most wonderful Daddy to our children, my soulmate and missing piece, had contracted bacterial meningococcal encephalitis — a rare form of meningitis that made my entire world collapse.

How did everyone else's world carry on?

The hollow space

Telling the children that Daddy hadn't made it, that Daddy had died, that he wouldn't be coming home, was the second worst thing I've ever had to do in my life.

The worst thing was — after signing all the paperwork — letting go of him at the doors of the operating theatre and saying my final goodbye as Pete donated his organs in a final act of kindness and generosity.

And then... thrown into grief. Survival mode. Planning some semblance of Christmas. Planning a cremation. Funeral directors, decisions I never thought I'd have to make. Building a Barbie house on Christmas Eve. Choosing photographs for a Celebration of Life. Pushing Christmas dinner round my plate and wondering why on earth we'd cooked a turkey. Choosing poems and writing a eulogy. Watching my daughter perform in her school nativity. Receiving sympathy cards and flowers. Making the kids packed lunches.

All so normal.

And all so far removed from normal that I felt like an alien in my own life.

Life carried on around me while I felt like I was sludging through treacle.

Looking back, I'm now truly grateful for the shock that allowed me to keep functioning. I'm thankful for survival mode kicking in and helping me get through.

The builders came in and caused chaos in my house for eight months with the extension Pete and I had talked about for so long.

I went away with my best friend and my girlfriends a few times that first year.

I stood and calmly told well-meaning people what had happened, without shedding a tear. Like I was talking about someone else, not me, not my husband. Disassociation of the highest order.

Our subconscious brain is so marvellously well equipped to protect us from emotional pain at all costs.

Early grief, to me, was like being underwater. You can still see, hear, and function — but it's not as clear as it is above the surface. Everything is dampened. Blurry. A bit murky. Harder to move.

Of course, there were moments when it was all-consuming and overwhelming. Ugly tears and superfluous snot featured highly.

Sometimes, with my best friend sitting alongside me. Mostly, alone in my bed at night, the kids safely tucked into bed, and me safe with my own big feelings after doing my best to help them with theirs.

And it was in bed, alone with my journal, that I would write to Pete in those early days. I'd get my feelings out onto the page and share all my thoughts with him. It was my way of remaining close to him, keeping our connection. And while it would never bring my husband back, it helped me feel he was near.

Signs and the sacred

A thoughtful friend, as soon as she'd heard about Pete dying, sent me a copy of a book in the post. The book was *Signs* by Laura Lynne Jackson. It's one of the few books I've been able to finish (grief took away my ability to focus on reading), and I devoured it. In the book, Laura shares stories of those who have passed away sending signs to their loved ones left behind.

It's my own personal belief that we are all energy and that our body is atoms, protons, and electrons, just as everything else we see and touch is (also what we can't necessarily see and touch). I know that Pete also believed this. We'd both read numerous books on theories like this, that our energy lives on after we're gone. Pete believed it and researched it from his scientist point of view. And I'd read it from a humanity and spiritual point of view. We'd had some really interesting discussions about it all, so it brought me comfort to know that wherever Pete was now, he was still with me in spirit, that his energy could still be with us.

After reading *Signs*, I asked Pete for a very specific one. I asked him to send me a missing piece. A jigsaw piece. Our sign. His name for me.

I'd seen the robins and feathers. Rainbows were a definite sign that I knew Pete sent to me regularly. But I wanted — no, NEEDED — him to send me something so specific to us that there could be no doubt it was him.

And I kept asking. I told him I didn't mind when, and that I understood it was a really hard brief, but that I had faith he'd deliver. There had never been a moment in our relationship when Pete hadn't delivered, so I knew without doubt that he would. And that when he did, it would be perfect.

Anyone else would have missed it.

One summer evening, out walking the dog with my daughter, there it was.

Tucked away, under a bush, almost invisible.

But to me it shone and sparkled so brightly that I knew instantly it was Pete. He'd sent me the sign.

Just like how I *knew* in my heart on The Day Everything Changed, I knew again.

My heart beat a little faster as I bent down to pick it up. Yes! A perfect jigsaw piece. All by itself. The missing piece, waiting for me. I popped it into my pocket and, not wanting to make a big fuss until I could get home and process this myself, I didn't say anything to my daughter.

The missing piece wasn't just a sign. It was so much more than that. It was a promise. A recognition of something that is so much bigger than us.

My missing piece was still with me. He always will be. Love never dies.

Redefining the puzzle

I'd discussed asking for a sign with my grief counsellor. I knew I needed something to help me process the trauma I'd been through, so I sought out counselling a few months after Pete died.

One of the things my counsellor kept repeating to me was how 'high functioning' I was. She encouraged me to allow myself to go into the grief, to give myself the space and time to be *in* the emotion of it all.

But with three children, in the midst of building work, trying to re-establish myself into work again, I simply didn't have the space to give myself that grace. Life was noisy, and I rarely had the time to sit with my thoughts, to process my feelings, or to allow myself to be in those moments where the grief would hit like a tidal wave.

And so, in the main, it got suppressed. Repressed. Pushed down.

I got told how strong I was. How amazing I was doing.

Meanwhile, I kept waiting for it to come and bite me on the backside.

And it did. Big time.

Sixteen months after Pete died, it was Mother's Day weekend — a weekend he'd always made special in recognition of me; a weekend we'd always spend doing something lovely together as a family. The first Mother's Day after his death had come and gone in a blur, so I can barely remember it. Much like most of that first 12-15 months.

So, this Mother's Day felt different. I wasn't looking forward to facing a weekend where the gaping void in our family was made even more stark with Pete's absence.

Saturday morning arrived, and I couldn't get out of bed. I felt like I'd been superglued to the mattress. It felt like more than just needing a bit of a lie-in; something wasn't quite right. When I didn't emerge for a while, my eldest came up to see me, and I think I managed to croak out something along the lines of me not being able to get up today... I could see the panic in his eyes as he urged me to get up, pleading with me and asking who was going to look after them if I didn't get up. At that point, in all honesty, I didn't care. All feeling had left my body.

The kids came in and out, and I could see their mouths moving but couldn't hear any words coming out. I heard something about calling 'Aunty Sarah' (my best friend) and then 'getting Granny over' (my mum).

And so the kids were rescued from my breakdown by the two people who have held me up since — my mum and my best friend.

That was the realisation that the grief was always going to come. Just not in weekly scheduled sessions.

Shortly after this episode where I was, quite literally, paralysed by my unprocessed grief, I booked myself in for a solo spa day. I think I needed it!

A day of sauna, steam, and cold plunge, with massage and journaling, was *exactly* what the doctor didn't order. And it was there, sitting in my robe with my trusty journal in front of me that I had the realisation (it had been whispering for a while) that I was here, that all of this grief, this lived experience, this wondering what the lessons might be, was to help others with their grief too.

If I'd been through this horrific experience of sudden loss, if I'd had to have the flashbacks on repeat of those few days surrounding Pete dying, then it was up to me to turn all that pain into a purpose.

I announced my new mission and was flooded with kind offers of support, people saying they knew I was destined for this mission and pointing me in the direction of others who might help.

First things first, though. I knew I had to fully process my own grief. I learned about Grief Edu-Therapy™ and signed up, not only to train as a grief specialist, but to go through the intense process of healing myself.

I realised I'm here to help make the world a more grief-literate place.

Having experienced others' awkwardness around what to say and do when someone has lost their loved one made me see that people need help in this area. Sharing my own story and my own grief journey made others feel seen too.

The piece that remains

I know that my amazing husband is with me and the wind beneath my wings in everything that I now do. He'd always say to me "go and change people's lives, Lou!" as I'd start a new coaching client or support someone.

We talk about him all the time at home. Sometimes still in the present tense. And that's OK. Because he *is* very much part of us. And always will be. He's very much alive in my heart and soul, and I can hear his voice, his dry humour, and his steadying words in everything I do.

We were supposed to spend the rest of our lives together. But I'm so incredibly glad he got to spend the rest of *his* life with me. And Pete will always be alongside me, always my missing piece.

That missing piece hasn't been replaced. It never could be. But I've begun to build around it. Post-traumatic growth, some would say. Focussing on how my own experience can help others indirectly helps me. Knowing I'm making a difference and knowing I'm making Pete proud, I'm using my grief for good and to fuel my bigger purpose. It allows it to move through me.

I often talk about the dualities of grief. The strange way that two seemingly conflicting emotions can co-exist. The 'and-also' of feeling deep intense sadness, *and also* the ability to feel awe, wonder, and the joy of being alive. The loneliness of knowing a part of me is missing forever, *and also* the knowledge that I am somehow more whole. The ability to notice the beauty and glimmers and be fully present in the moment, *and also* a full-bodied knowing that we aren't guaranteed tomorrow.

Life is for the taking. No need to ask for permission. It's already yours.

Dedication:

My amazing Pete, this chapter is for you. Someone asked me if I'd rather not have had the ten-and-a-half years we spent together if it meant I didn't have to go through this emotional pain of losing you. And my answer, in every lifetime, would be never. Whilst our time together was so relatively short, every single moment, day, and year with you was exquisite. I can't help but wonder if on some subconscious soul level, we knew our time together was limited. Perhaps that's why we didn't waste a single moment. I will never stop loving you, talking about you and to you. Until our souls and hearts meet again, your missing piece, Lou xxx

Biography:

Lou Hynes' world was turned upside down when her husband took himself to bed feeling unwell, and only a few hours later she was left a widow. He had contracted bacterial meningitis, which caused such serious swelling to his brain that it killed him within hours. In the aftermath of this devastation, she experienced for herself how uncomfortable we are around grief and decided to turn her pain into purpose.

Lou's mission is now to help create a more grief-literate society so that grievers can feel supported with compassion and not awkwardness. She does this using her experience as a coach, hypnotherapist, and her Grief Edu-Therapy™ training to run Grief Education Workshops for businesses, give keynote talks, as well as offering one-to-one grief support for those wishing to navigate their own emotional pain. She lives in Leeds and is mum to her three children and their dog, Rosie.

You can connect with Lou here:

https://linktr.ee/louhynes

Uncle Brian

– My Father Figure and Best Friend
By Emily Nuttall

"We run from grief because loss scares us, yet our hearts reach towards grief because the broken parts want to mend. C. S. Lewis wrote, 'No one ever told me that grief felt so like fear.' We can't rise strong when we're on the run."

– Brené Brown,

Content warning: mentions sensitive subjects. If you are struggling, please see resources and helplines included in this chapter for support, or contact your GP.

It was a sunny summer's afternoon in Guernsey, the Channel Islands, on Friday, the 7th of July, 2023, and I was lying flat like a star at my safe place called Bordeaux beach and harbour. Surrounding me was tall green grass, with daisies growing through, and colourful butterflies landing on them.

I lay there, fully visualising the crispy yellow sand and stones on the beach in front of me, watching the dogs running freely, the views of the rockery, the picturesque image of the Vale Castle, the sight of the beautiful bright blue sea, and all the boats docked in Bordeaux harbour. With my eyes wide open, I was contentedly taking in the sounds of the waves crashing and hitting the big rocks on the beach, the noises of the young children running around, screaming and laughing, the sounds of the crows and seagulls squawking away, dogs barking and chasing tennis balls. And in the background, I could hear the sound of the coffee machine coming from the kiosk, with people chattering whilst awaiting their food and drinks.

I then turned my gaze upwards, into the beautiful bright blue sky, yellow sunshine, and bold white clouds that shone brightly over the other Channel Islands of Sark and Hern. I mindfully started to make different shapes and pictures out of the clouds, imagining the next magical story they would take me on as they glided along in the sky.

As I lay there, suddenly I could terrifyingly feel my body start to jerk and shake, followed by a tear drop down my face which then turned into a river of relentless tears. I quickly scrunched my face up, closed my eyes, and tried hard to curl up and hide myself in the long grass so that no-one would notice or see. I so desperately hoped that the overpowering washing machine of flashbacks, visions, and painful reminders that were coming violently into my mind would stop.

On that exact date just seven months earlier – on the morning of the 7th of December, 2022 – my world devastatingly, unexpectedly, and painfully came crashing down like a ton of bricks. For the five days prior to that date, I had been stuck in isolation, coping and healing from a second round of Covid; from an unexpected accident whilst at my safe haven of Bordeaux on Saturday, 26th November; and also slowly rebuilding and healing from a failed, secretive, painful, and traumatic suicide attempt on my life on Tuesday, 15th November. During this whole traumatic, lonely, hopeless time, I had been in touch daily with my Uncle Brian.

I had experienced the devastating sudden and unexpected losses of my three previous role models in my life, in 2008, 2012, and 2019 – one of whom was my Gran Molly, who was a petite lady with grey curly hair. She was an incredible primary school and music teacher, patient and caring, and I trusted her with what I was experiencing at my father and stepmother's house. The relationship with my own mother was broken, and I was lost, angry, scared, and going off the rails. But Gran, with her calming nature and words, was always close by, like a guardian angel on my shoulder hugging me. She would keep me safe, making everything ok. And together with my mental health, eating disorder, disability and family intervention teams, she held everything together.

My Nan Chris was a fitness fanatic, energetic, smiling lady, who had very curly brown hair, an infectious smile that would make me feel better, and gave the best hugs in the world. This allowed me to feel loved and comforted, as if I was being hugged by my brown, fluffy teddy bear. As I was so young and trying to make sense of the world, Nan was patient and would listen openly, never letting me give up, no matter what the challenge may have been with my physical disability. Most importantly, she believed in me, helping me grow through disability sports, enabling me to feel included within society.

And finally, my Aunt Meg – my musical inspiration and a teacher. She was petite but had a warming voice. She helped me to understand and make sense of the world. She encouraged and inspired my creative talents, helping me to develop into a confident, intellectual woman through writing, music, dance, and art. Like Gran and Nan, she kept the family together and me safe from harm, helping me to achieve anything I set my mind to. They all helped me to make sense of the world I was living in and gave me hope for my eating disorder, mental health, disability, and addiction recovery.

Uncle Brian was musically talented, artistically creative, and attempted to be sporty; he was a superhero that I looked up to. He had become my father figure, the rock, and the glue to me and the rest of the family, my go-to, and my best friend. He had instilled the memories of my gran, nan, and aunt, so that they were never forgotten and the amazing things they had offered me could be continued to be brought to life in as many ways as possible. He helped to remind me that even though they were gone, they were still there somewhere in all that he did with me and in all areas and aspects of my life, connections, and relationships. I was forever thankful and grateful to have the opportunity to keep on building, growing, and making their support an essential part of the challenging, painful, difficult, but appreciative and opportunistic life I could truly have, no matter what.

I remember it was at 10.30pm on the night of Tuesday, 6th December, 2022. Every night at the same time, I would eagerly grab my mobile phone and hold the speed dial number one down on my phone, which had my uncle's mobile number saved into it. We would have an end-of-night chat, talk about our days, how each of us was feeling, discussing any of my physical, mental health, addiction, or life struggles, our shared love for piano, guitar, singing, and writing poetry. We'd share thoughts on our weekly picturesque adventures at Bordeaux and other completely random conversations that made the calls even more special, even if he had already called or sometimes visited me at some other point that day.

Normally, I'd have to only wait for one ring to be greeted by an eager "Hello, Em" in a funny voice. I would have to try and work out which character it was from one of our favourite cartoons. Or something completely random would greet me, and we would just end up in fits of laughter even before we had begun our call together.

But on this particular night, the phone just kept on ringing. And after ten rings, it just went to voicemail. At first, I wasn't particularly concerned, as my uncle was known for his regular enjoyable little mid-afternoon "power naps" that would often turn into nearly an all-night sleep. Or sometimes he'd leave his phone on silent if he'd been out teaching, giving lifts to his best friend, or volunteering during the day and just needed some peace and quiet. And with his technological skills being non-existent, he had probably not heard his mobile or not known how to change it back to being on the loud setting from silent. When this happened, once he had figured out the problem, he would always say, "I want to throw this damn phone into orbit."

As I was starting to get tired, I made one last attempt, but again there was no answer. In this situation, I would usually call my mum, as she and my uncle were now next-door neighbours. After ringing my mum, who also didn't answer – which was normal – I started calling around my cousins, but their phones were also going straight to voicemail.

Having had previous family experiences when I would contact them at planned/arranged times and not getting a response after several attempts, it usually meant that something unexpected, painful, traumatic, or difficult had happened. I immediately got that horrible feeling in my stomach, like a grumbling, churning feeling, and my mind started racing at 100 miles an hour. I was starting to imagine every possible worst-case scenario: Have they had an accident? Is someone unwell, ill, dead, or injured? Has there been a family falling out that I am not aware of?

I spent the next hour, till nearly midnight, just pacing my bedroom. I was still feeling horrendously unwell physically with Covid, and mentally I was already struggling, and my mind couldn't stop. But in the end, my exhausted body and mind gave up, and I must have just naturally fallen asleep.

When I woke the following day at around 6.45am, I instantly checked my phone – still nothing.

Around 30 minutes later, my phone moved around and vibrated with its bold ringtone, and I eagerly grabbed it, thinking it would be my uncle calling to apologise for missing my call and laughing his head off that his power nap had turned into an all-night sleep. He had also just got over Covid, and for the past few weeks and months had said he felt like he had been hit by a bus. He'd put it down to exhaustion from work, Covid, and catching various infections and viruses which were all going around at the same time.

The call, though, wasn't my uncle. I didn't have a chance to look at the number ringing, so I just answered. But before I could say anything, I heard some brief muffling, then the voice of a tearful, distressed girl on the end of the phone. As she was so upset, I did not initially realise it was my cousin Ellie. And all I could hear her keep mumbling through her sobs was, "I'm sorry. I'm so sorry."

My initial thought was perhaps she was apologising for ignoring my call the night before, or maybe she was over-tired from working and looking after the children. Often when we spoke, she would be either happy, sad, stressed, and tearful, or a mixture of them all, and keen to share something embarrassing or daft she had done, or just to have a good old rant.

This time, I didn't have time to say a usual proper hello or to ask her what was wrong. Instead, she just blurted out, "Uncle Brian is in hospital, we've been here all night. He is very poorly… I don't think we have long left with him, I'm afraid, my darling. I need to go, as the nurse is coming, but as soon as she has left, I will call you straight back." Then the phone went dead.

My mind a whirl of thoughts, I just remember saying aloud, "She's lying, this isn't happening. This is a horrible dream that I've woken from; one of my favourite fairytale stories that's gone horribly wrong."

For the next hour I just sat in a completely numb daze on the end of my bed, staring out my bedroom window. The world and the clouds were just spinning at 100 miles per hour.

When the phone finally rang again, I eagerly grabbed it, hoping she had woken from a daft dream and was ready to tell me the story. However, this time she was sobbing hysterically.

"I'm sorry. I'm so, so sorry, my darling," she managed, "but Uncle Brian has passed away peacefully, with me, Peter, Hugh, Jonah, your mum, and Rod by his hospital bedside, at 8am this morning."

I dropped the phone to the floor whilst it was still on the call and fell onto my knees. Curling up into a ball, I screamed, "Shut up! Shut up! Please tell me this isn't happening. Make it all go away. Let this nightmare be over and everything back to normal."

Too distressed to hear her voice any longer, and fearful I might say something angry that I'd later regret, I grabbed the phone and ended the call. Then I threw the phone across the room and lay on the floor, rocking and curling up into my knees, screaming and sobbing into them so no-one could hear my desperate cries. I kept begging for it all to stop so that I could be numb, to shut down and pretend nothing had just happened.

The hours and next few days went by as a complete blur. I was still stuck in isolation with Covid for another six days. Stuck in my own lonely, scary, confusing head, twenty-four seven. I just wanted to be disconnected; I just wanted to not feel anything. But suddenly things were moving on quickly.

I was having virtual phone calls with the family and then the vicar from my uncle's local church four days later. Having to think about the funeral arrangements, the family flowers, how the service might want to look in line with my uncle's wishes, the music, and the readings to be used, the transport, the after event, the tributes to think about and his life story. And after the funeral conversations, the discussions of my uncle's money, where it would go, how it would be shared, what we would receive as his nieces, nephews, and family members from his Will. Thinking about having to clear out his house and look through his treasured possessions, about what we would want to hold onto for the special memories. Everything was suddenly thrown my way to think about, and it was like an overwhelm bucket pouring out faster than it was being refilled.

I was also asked if I would be willing to write a poem in my uncle's memory and to share it at the funeral, which was an opportunity I was grateful to be given. My cousin Ellie was tasked with having to write and bring together the family tributes and memories, which she would be talking about and sharing.

As soon as I was alone in my bedroom after these meetings and calls, I began work on the poem I wanted to write and share for my uncle's funeral. The mask of "I'm fine, brave, and strong" came fully off. And it was replaced with painful, secretive, haunting voices from my childhood, teenage years of emotional abuse, violence, homelessness, family breakdowns I had gone through with my father, stepmother, and other family members, and other violent relationships.

Having gone through these other traumatic losses of my gran, nan, and aunt, I was also still experiencing several mental health struggles in this period of time, with eating disorders, self-harm, depression, autism, my physical health, disabilities, many surgeries, and suicidal thoughts and attempts. Although much of this had been known about in my journey for the last fourteen years, I also had a secret gambling addiction that no-one knew nothing about. It's something I have been struggling with, even now.

For so long, many forms of release, numbness, punishment, and escapism have consumed me with utter desperation and terrifying urges, as though I was being crushed by a ton of bricks and locked inside a washing machine in my own head.

The voices of my past and my inner child secretly and hauntingly started to come back into my mind when I was in my bedroom, and even to this day they scream at me: "You didn't deserve to write anything to share about your uncle. You weren't there when he died, like he had always been there for you through all your mental health, gambling, eating disorder, self-harm addictions, traumas, rehab, in-patient admissions, medical hospital admissions, disabilities, surgeries, struggles, suicidal thoughts and attempts, pains and fears. This is your fault. You are a selfish, horrible person, and you need to be ashamed of yourself. You don't deserve the safe places and special memories you created with your uncle at Bordeaux. You don't deserve your helping and community talents, or your artistic talents, your poetic talents, your singing, guitar or piano-playing skills and opportunities, your writing, studying, working opportunities. You deserve to punish yourself. You should have been the one to die on the 15th November, 2022, after your failed suicide attempt, instead of him.

"You don't deserve any of his Will. Get rid of it, as you deserve absolutely nothing from losing your uncle, just like all the other sudden traumatic losses that were your fault – your gran, nan, and aunt – and the compensation money from your disabilities because of your loss of vision in your left eye, and the money you had left from them and these experiences that you have shamefully gambled away. This is your mess once again, and now you deserve to lose everything in all areas of your life for good, and you deserve to be forever gone."

With these feelings, experiences, and beliefs, my way of coping from my loss of my uncle is my ongoing gambling addiction, mental health and disability recovery, and the journey of understanding that I am on. And to this day, coming to terms with the sudden, traumatic, and unexpected loss of my uncle is something I am still affected by and having to navigate.

I'm still bravely dealing with this and removing the "I'm fine" mask that has kept me safe and protected.

With the right understanding, treatments, trauma therapies, and support, I am constantly grounding myself and taking myself back to my favourite place in Bordeaux, the sea, the grass, daisies, dogs, beach, butterflies, the boats, the sounds of the children, the Vale Castle, and the birds. The ability to be able to sun gaze, cloud watch, and make stories, brings me close to my uncle. It is a safe, free place where I can feel connected to him. Even when it's painfully hard, dark, lonely, and scary, it's the light, the hope that I desperately try and hold onto.

Yes, my uncle isn't sitting there with me in this place, but his spirit and my other lost loved ones' spirits are my guardian angels on my shoulders, holding me, loving me, comforting me, and protecting me. And that brings me peace, light, connection, and hope in light of the loss, darkness, despair, and pain. And it reminds me he is still there watching me, willing me on, believing in me, and opening my world up every day to new opportunities and experiences creatively, emotionally, through my many working, helping, volunteering roles, and through my musical and art talents. His inspiration and being my encourager and role model in this will never leave my side, and for that

I will forever be thankful and grateful. And this empowers and inspires me to give strength and hope to others every single day.

A Poem in Memory of Uncle Brian

Uncle Brian. Creative, imaginative, caring, loving, are some of my four powerful words to describe an uncle like you.

Your artistic and imaginative talent always shining through.

Together we used to sit for hours, doing all different types of drawing, sharing stories, going through family photos, and being out exploring.

Scrabble games and crosswords we would do together and complete, even through the frustration with words and clues and the tapping of your feet. I would refer to this as the special Uncle Brian beat.

There was never a dull moment in the days we spent together; the smallest things that would make us laugh what felt like forever, whether that was one of your commentary trips from you driving me home or to an appointment in the car! With some of the sayings you would come out with being hilarious and quite bizarre.

Or the times I'd see you desperate to throw your phone and technology into orbit afar. The smile on your face you would show when you were doing these things, with gritted teeth, sharing one of your regular sayings at the same time whilst in fits of laughter, which was "Good grief".

The hilarious and amazing presents you used to like to buy for me, whether that was a Perry's map when I would often get lost somewhere around Guernsey, or a Sellotape holder to unstick my ravelled-up mess, or a dictionary for word definitions to get me through assignment stress.

But that's what made you the amazing unique special Uncle Brian, that no matter what, you were always there with open arms, love, and care.

Our daily conversations we would always have, which reminded me throughout my many struggles I was never alone, because you were always there both in person and on the other end of the phone.

Now, since your sudden passing, it hasn't quite sunk in. So much having to be processed, where do I even begin?

But I know you're no longer suffering, or in pain, but free and at peace, and that brings me so much comfort and relief.

You inspired me to work hard and always make you proud, and whenever it feels tough, I'll just look up in the clouds.

Whenever I hear the birds sing or see the butterflies fly by, I will feel your presence falling down from the sky.

I know there will be days without you that I will feel lost, upset, and sad. But I have to thank you, Uncle Brian, for being there, teaching me, inspiring me, guiding me, and for being the best uncle I'm so grateful I could have ever had.

Now you can lie peacefully free of your suffering and pain, I know that one day we will be together again.

I know you, Auntie Meg, Granny Molly, and Nanny Chris will always be watching from afar, and you will always be my brightest shining stars.

Dedication:

I dedicate this chapter to all those on a journey of painful loss, grief, and having to understand the world around them after losing someone they so dearly love. I promise you are not alone, even when it might feel you are the only one going through this at the time. There will always be someone to hold your hand and walk alongside you, listen and understand you. Coping, dealing, and coming to terms with grief is not a race, and we all cope and experience it differently and take different lengths of time to get through it. But I promise you there is support and understanding out there, through friends, family, charities, therapies, and helplines, and ways to build your toolbox of coping safely, creatively, and positively. Be brave to reach out for help, keep your loved one's legacies alive in all you do and all they did with you. It will keep you connected and close, empower and inspire others, as well as support your healing journey. Remember, it is ok to remove your mask and ask for help. Sending love, light, strength, and hope. All my love Emily x

Biography:

Emily Nuttall is a trainee counsellor who's just completed her Level 3. She's an expert by experience, advisory board member for Eating Disorders, lived experience lead for the King's Transitions eating disorders youth intervention project, an inspirational speaker, trainer, and project worker, an inspiring individual who's overcome many adversities with her lived experiences of anorexia, depression, self-harm, anxiety, autism, traumas, disabilities, suicide, emotional abuse, homelessness, gambling addiction, and family breakdowns. She works, coaches, speaks, trains, and delivers projects as an expert by experience in the areas of neurodiversity, autism, eating disorders, self-harm, suicide, disabilities, education, and trauma, with many organisations. These include the States of Guernsey Autism, Mental Health, Education and Eating Disorder Services for both children and adults; Beat, the UK eating disorders charity; Freed; Peace Pathway, Guernsey; UK Mind; Samaritans; Guernsey Mobility Let's Go; Grassroots Suicide Prevention; EDAC; EDCRN; King's College, Maudsley, and other NHS trusts; CEDS; PEDS; Family Action, Autism Bedfordshire; Action for Children; Birmingham University; Bournemouth University. She also delivers projects and training independently with her Motivate the Mind business in these areas. Emily's a co-author of 12 books, a volunteer disability sports coach, and a mentor with several services, communities, and charities, empowering and inspiring long-lasting change.

You can connect with Emily here:
https://linktr.ee/emilyn93

Who am I?

My Journey to Soft Nursing By Ashleigh Quick

"Courage isn't only fighting our circumstances, sometimes making peace with our circumstances requires more courage."
– Tori Amos

Nearly all of us have experienced grief in one way or another. Grief is defined as an experience towards coping with a loss, generally the death of a loved one. Grief incorporates physiological distress and can include feelings such as distress, separation anxiety, confusion, yearning, and apprehension about the future.

During my nursing career we learnt about the stages of grief by Elisabeth Kübler Ross in her 1969 book, *On Death and Dying*, which was based on her work with terminally ill patients. Although grief is a nonlinear process, the five stages we tend to go through are: denial; anger; bargaining; depression; and acceptance.

These have since grown into the seven stages of grief: shock and denial; pain and guilt; anger and bargaining; depression; the upward turn; reconstruction and working through; and acceptance and hope. These are the common emotional patterns most of us feel through grief, though we must bear in mind this is not universal, and all our experiences are individual and personal. As humans, we may also experience them in a different order.

We must also bear in mind the physical manifestation of grief, such as fatigue, digestive issues, muscle tension, and even tightness of the chest. It is not just our heart that feels deep pain, but our stomach, throat, changes in our appetite and sleep patterns.

Grief takes an enormous toll on our bodies, both physically and mentally. It is a common but difficult life experience, to which most people successfully adapt. However, some can also have what is called complicated grief – an ongoing feeling of yearning or longing for something that is no longer present, intense loneliness, a feeling that life is unbearable, and frequent thoughts of our loss. This can generally last longer than 12 months and may require additional professional help. Support is crucial here.

What if grief wasn't just about losing a loved one? What if it can occur in other aspects of our lives? Grief is a natural emotional response to loss, any loss. It is a deeply personal experience which can be felt differently for all of us.

Since working as a chemotherapy nurse practitioner for 30 years, I have certainly seen my fair share of death and grief. It is also a feeling I had from a very early age, after losing my father to leukaemia when I was just nine. I know now that as a child I did not know what grief was, I was just sad that my daddy wasn't here anymore. By aged 11, I had lost my grandmother, and I can remember this loss as pain and anger. Who else was going to leave me in this huge wide world?

Adjusting to life without someone or something in our lives is an intense feeling, but over time it usually becomes less tense. Grief can also be felt by someone with a long-term illness, or a terminal diagnosis. Or maybe the loss of a family pet.

Grief and the experience of loss can be triggered by any event that disrupts our sense of normalcy or self. This can be linked to the loss of a home or job, but it can also arise from the loss of health. The latter can be a significant source of grief and is known as loss of physical health.

For me, grief struck again when I had to walk away from a career I had dedicated 30 years of my life to, a job that had offered me absolute satisfaction, a job that defined me. It was my identity, my soul purpose, after being a mother.

Anticipatory grief is a feeling of sadness, worry, or anger about a potential future loss, which is often associated with a lifelong terminal illness. I have witnessed this myself many times in my career. It occurs in response to a change in our lives that cause a sense of loss, or a change in identity.

I now want to focus on my own personal journey. Not just as a nurse, but as me, as I am human too. Many years ago, when my children were of primary school age, I was suffering with excessive lethargy and pain in nearly every joint in my body. My son would ask to go to the park, but my body just couldn't move off the sofa without immense pain. I would get frustrated and angry at myself.

I repeatedly presented with a chest infection month after month, was prescribed antibiotics again and again, ending up in A&E over and over, put on nebulisers to help me breathe. I had difficulty sleeping. Light became my tormentor; it was unbearable. I began living in darkness, but at the time I hadn't realised how closed off to daylight I had become. I became clumsy, and I would have days of low mood.

After attending the doctors for what seemed like the hundredth time, they finally – after two years – agreed to refer me to the Rheumatology department at my local hospital. I can also assure you, nurses are not given special treatment to jump queues!

I remember thinking, *I'm sure this will be another waste of time.* As I sat in the waiting room, looking around, what struck me was how young I felt in comparison to the other patients with their walking sticks or arriving to the department in a wheelchair and being helped to sit down. I felt like a fraud. A type of imposter syndrome, doubting my own illness and symptoms. My thoughts ran wild: *Maybe my symptoms aren't real, maybe I'm just worse at dealing with them than other people are. I need to exercise more, eat better. I just shouldn't be here; others need help far more than I do.*

I heard my name being called. *Ok, let's just get this over with.* I remember following the short doctor into the consulting room. We spoke for a while, discussing my medical history, symptoms, and a little about my personal life. He then asked if I had had a traumatic event before these symptoms started. Let's just say, yes, and it involved a man.

"Do you mind if I do a physical examination," he asked with his kind almost childlike smile and pearly white teeth. *Go for it*, I thought, *you won't find anything*. He began feeling the glands in my neck, listening to my chest. *Nothing new here*, I thought, *the GP has done that a thousand times*. How critical I was at this point. He began testing the movement of my joints, how he could turn my legs in what felt like a very odd direction. I thought, *Whose legs bend sideways anyway?*

He asked me to sit up, and when he pushed an area on my shoulders, the pain was excruciating, I felt a hot flash across my face, then he pressed another point and another, all over my body. And every spot made me hotter and hotter; the intensity one of his tiny little fingers could make was unreal. He finished, and I was glad it was all over.

"Take a seat," he said.

I sat down thinking, *It's hot in here*. My heart was still pounding in my chest, like a horse galloping across the fields.

"You have fibromyalgia and hypermobility syndrome," he informed me. "You must rest and take pain relief when required. We will see you again in six months, but in the meantime, I would like you to have some bloods taken."

Rest. Rest? I thought, *I have two children under seven, who I raise myself. I work and have a house to run. And you want me to rest?*

I went straight away for my bloods, then I drove home, where my mother was with my two children. I told her what the doctor had said, then I just got on with the rest of my day. It wasn't until a few days later that I felt a sense of wonder and, intrigued, I began to research these two conditions.

Fibromyalgia is a chronic condition characterised as pain throughout the body and generally accompanied by fatigue and sleep disturbance. *That about sums it up*, I thought. The symptoms I had first described all related to this one condition. So, I went on to search hypermobility syndrome, also known as Joint Hypermobility Syndrome (JHS). This is a condition characterised by excessive flexibility and range of movement in multiple joints, also causing pain, stiffness, and fatigue. I've always been rather bendy.

A few months passed, during which I didn't really rest more but carried on with my pain relief. Sleep and tiredness remained the same. A letter came earlier than expected, asking me to attend Rheumatology again.

I went in straight away and we spoke for a little while then came to my blood test results. I was informed I had Systemic Sclerosis, which I had never heard of before. *Something new to research*, I thought. We talked a little about it, but for some reason when I left the consulting room, my mind went blank when he told me to go home and discuss it with my family and ensure I had good support when I told my children. *Odd*, I thought, and brushed it aside.

I didn't seem to ask any questions, but just sat quietly and tried to take it all in. I now know that I had switched off when he said life expectancy was five years – ten at the most. I'm now pushing around 15, and I'm not going anywhere yet.

I was immediately started on medication, immunosuppressants, to dampen down my immune system. I was also told I would be referred to the Autoimmune Disease Centre at the Royal Free Hospital in London for some more detailed tests.

I drove home, sat down with a lovely cup of tea, and began to research this condition. Bam! It hit me like I had just hooked a 40lb carp on the end of my ever-so-small 10ft rods and lost it. I read and I read until I couldn't see any more through the tears.

"When we sense a boundary of time, our curiosity awakes, and so do our desires for knowledge."
– Morhaf Al Achkar

Now began my first cycle of grief – utter denial the following day. *They must have it wrong*, I told myself. *I'm too young. What about my children? There is no cure.* The ultimate question hit me, *Why me?*

Being diagnosed with a serious medical condition can cause a sense of loss. Grief in its most general definition is an emotional reaction to significant loss, or change. When we traditionally think about grief, one automatically thinks about the death of a loved one, or the loss of a relationship. In that type of grief, the individual works through the grief, eventually accepts loss, and moves forward, having dealt with a common life experience that we must all eventually face.

Those living with a rare and chronic illness also experience grief and loss in a non-linear way. There is generally an identifiable beginning, and for me it was at time of diagnosis. But I wonder where the end might be.

There have certainly been emotional highs and lows along the way, usually coinciding with new or worsening symptoms, or changes in medication. This appears to complicate my ability to process things and often ends with a feeling of confusion, frustration, self-doubt, and feeling low. I have certainly experienced loss of my own identity, physically and mentally. My vision of life has looked distorted for the long term.

It is a little bit like shiny object syndrome, flitting from one thing to the next. It's a feeling of being lost at sea when you can see land and it vanishes again into the misted waters. Mostly, it's an emotional rollercoaster of highs and lows. A realisation I soon came to was that I could no longer become or maintain who I was as an individual.

The largest impact my illness has had to date was in 2024 when I made a call to my manager. I remember the words, and they still cut deep.

"Hi Michelle, how are you? I think the time has come to leave my job. I'm not safe anymore, and I don't think I would be able to undertake cardiac compressions if I had to."

With that, I broke down. I couldn't speak.

She just said, "Take your time, I'm here."

I finally stopped crying, we spoke some more, and the support I felt that day was amazing. In a way I felt relief. I no longer would have to struggle to open IV bags, to snap glass ampules, to cannulate, to just get through the day.

I was fortunate that another position came up in the company which I accepted. But then I hit the turmoil of feeling an utter failure

– to myself, my family, and wholeheartedly to my patients. I love each one of them.

And my journey with grief began once again...

Coping with a chronic illness and grief, we must firstly look and identify what it is exactly that we are grieving. What is the source of that grief? It takes time to validate and accept the loss, and for some it may be weeks, months, and may even take years.

At first, I needed to identify who I was: a chemotherapy nurse practitioner, mother, partner, or someone new. We are often seen by our accomplishments and achievements, but I just felt I had lost every piece of that part of me. *Was I now a disabled person on a sinking ship? No job prospects. I will never hold that patient's hand again; I will never hug the families and hold them tight.* My heart broke into pieces, and in all honesty, I'm still repairing that fractured part of me. Both work and recreational activities have been snatched away overnight. *Who am I?*

Odd as it may seem, humans need to mourn the losses to enable us to validate what working – or fishing, in my case – once provided. It's important to be grateful for those experiences, even though they may now be gone.

It's a time to make new plans, and to remind ourselves of all the things we can do. Maybe fishing can still be on the agenda. By applying modifications, I will be back on the bank, I can promise you that. My health now prevents me from so many outdoor activities, and I can no longer run. But I can walk. Just think of all the things I missed when running, how much more wildlife I will now be able to see. I think a new camera is on the agenda.

We must focus on the parts of our identities we still have – as a mother of both human and the furry form; daughter; partner; friend.

And I will always be a nurse, as it inside of me, part of me. It is my identity.

Something I've still yet to tackle and overcome is friendships; I don't want to be a burden on anyone. Also support systems – not necessarily for myself, but to support others, and the fact I can no longer be that person. Roles are starting to change. I am so tired daily, and I see my mother less than I used to, as days off for me are sacred. But, on the other hand, she is lonely, and I could help fill that void if I wasn't so tired all the time.

It's about finding ways to cope with the changes we face having a long-term illness. Who is around for support? Not everyone remains in our lives and must be a part of all our life journey. I have found new friends and new support networks since changing jobs. I also, for the first time, work alongside others with similar needs and challenges, who understand – truly understand. It's amazing connecting with others who "just get it". I think for family and friends who are well, they are unable to truly connect with the complexities of living with a chronic health condition. So, shared experiences can be validating and supportive. There are so many groups now where you can meet someone who shares your health condition, and in some cases, you don't even have to leave the sofa.

Having to change jobs absolutely threw me into occupational grief, and it was devastating. I was one of those people who loved my job, every part of it. I never woke up and thought, *I don't want to go to work today*. So, I think the sudden change in health which meant I had to change jobs left me questioning my identity as a nurse practitioner, but I also lost an entire community of patients. Patients I had seen more often than friends and even family, and my team. Although I was solo working, my team and manager were amazing. So, I felt I had lost so much. This is known as layered grief.

But what if all that change was a blessing, hiding behind those thoughts of failure? What if I could have a better quality of life? What if working from home would provide more flexibility, pain relief, more energy, or less stress? What if I'd have the time to focus on other areas of my life, ones I had neglected for so long?

It takes strength and perseverance, organisation and skill, to manage a chronic health condition. Every single day is different. You become your own medical secretary with great organisational skills. When you feel grief about your chronic illness, remember these skills and be proud of these accomplishments.

On the other hand, it's about not having the freedom to choose what you do. Planning goes out the window, as you never know how you are going to feel three weeks from now. Being unable to spend time with those you love at life events and occasions; those memories can be the hardest grief to come to terms with. Chronic illness steals this from us.

As I write this, I am grieving my own loss, looking back at all those events and memories I've missed. No-one wants to miss out on life because we don't feel well. This is not just a one-off circumstance; it happens time and time again, and it's an endless grief of frustration. We need to take time out to remember and remind ourselves that it is normal to grieve those losses and that our conditions are unpredictable.

Through a lot of personal work, with the help of family and friends, I realised I was grieving. That realisation allowed me to move through the anger and sadness and into acceptance. Acceptance doesn't mean that I don't still experience all those feelings, or that the process is easier. But it allows me to let go of the things I think my body should be or do, embracing it instead for what is now – brokenness and all.

I now accept and acknowledge that my losses and grief will always hurt, and experiencing grief is part of living with a rare and chronic health condition. All of us will grieve the loss of the friendships we were not able to repair, the holidays and weekends fishing we will never get back, and I wish every single day for a body that functions, one hour pain-free to enable me to carry out just one task without grimacing.

I share this grief with every one of you suffering today with a rare and/or chronic illness. I acknowledge and honour your daily struggles, your resilience, and your strength.

"My brain says let's do something exciting today, and my body says don't listen to that fool."
– Unknown

Dedication:

To my daughter who has supported me over the years, who treats me with respect and dignity, who has taught me about grace, strength, and kindness, standing strong together as you travel your own journey with a long-term health condition. I thank you and love you. I will continue to listen, advise, and support you through life – no judgements made, just a loving friendship for life. xxx

Biography:

Ashleigh Quick is a mother of two beautiful children – a boy and a girl, now aged 20 and 23 – and is extremely proud of them both. Ashleigh qualified as a nurse in 1996, then went on to study a Degree and Masters in Oncology and Palliative Care. She has worked as a Chemotherapy Nurse Specialist for almost 30 years. During her spare time, she enjoys carp fishing, yoga, walking, reading, and spending quiet time with her family. Ashleigh has always seen herself as an empath and stives to put others first. She thrives on learning new things and qualified as an NLP Practitioner and Hypnotherapist during 2020-2022. Most recently, she undertook training to become a Certified Grief Coach and is currently studying to become a counsellor.

Ashleigh has always been passionate about helping others. She has a free FB group where she offers a different yet powerful approach to managing low self-esteem, boosting confidence by unveiling those doubts. By offering a natural approach, she also helps people with chronic pain, unwanted chemotherapy side effects, and teaching coping strategies for those living with an ongoing chronic illness. Ashleigh herself has been a chronic pain sufferer for many years and was shown the power of NLP and Hypnosis to relieve symptoms. This led to her forming her own path to help others as she has been helped. She also assists families with the difficult task of talking to their children regarding life-limiting conditions and the potential outcome.

The Silence That Follows
By Kari Roberts

"Grief is the price we pay for love."
– Queen Elizabeth II

Content warning: This chapter mentions child loss.

There's a particular kind of grief that lives in the quiet. Not loud or dramatic, but heavy like the air has changed suddenly. It sits deep in your bones, and it lingers in doorways. This followed me home from the hospital, along with my empty arms, and it stayed with me forever.

When a baby dies, it's not just a life that's lost; it's a future that was already unfolding in your mind. A thousand tiny moments you had counted on, sleepless nights, soft breathing in the night when they finally sleep and you hold your breath, the curve of a cheek against your chest, first steps, first birthdays, a voice calling your name.

I have experienced loss before and after the death of my second son Stanley. My biological father, after getting to know him again, died suddenly; my mother died during the lockdown after the pandemic;

and my stepfather faded away after Mum died – all bringing their own but very different experiences. Grief can feel all-consuming, grief can feel numb, and sometimes grief feels like relief, but the guilt that brings stops us talking about it. Funny that the only two things guaranteed in our life are birth and death, and death is something so many shy away from talking about.

There is no hierarchy in grief. Some say losing a child is the worst form of loss, then it depends on their age, and the list of what's better or worse goes on. Grief is grief, no better, no worse, and with no dilution of anyone's experience.

Writing this chapter has been tough, much tougher than I expected, and there are times I thought it wouldn't get finished. Even writing this, I am wondering if I will complete the chapter.

Even now, years later, grief still finds its way in. It doesn't knock. It doesn't ask permission. It simply bursts in.

And yet, like the tide, I've learned to move with it. Sometimes crashing, sometimes calm, and always there. Writing this has been like learning to breathe underwater – uncomfortable, disorienting, and strangely beautiful.

There are countless theories and models about grief, how it's supposed to look, how long it's supposed to last. Experts will challenge each other and change their views after years of more research. But this chapter isn't about any of that.

This is about my grief, my story, my son, and how his life ended before it even began. It's about what happens in the moments no-one prepares you for, the silence that follows, the empty arms, the ache that settles in your bones. It's about what I still carry quietly and always will.

If you're holding your own kind of grief, loud or silent, I hope this chapter helps you feel seen. Not fixed. Not hurried. Just understood.

It happens so fast, the folding in of a world that had only just begun to open. One moment, there is anticipation, preparation, a rush of emotion... and the next, silence. Not the kind that soothes but the kind that hollows.

Stanley died thirty-eight years ago. My second pregnancy all seemed to be going smoothly until labour started at thirty-nine weeks. It was a Good Friday, 17th April, 1987. The delivery room was busy, but nothing out of the ordinary seemed to happen until he was born, and then things got scary.

He took his first breath and then struggled until taking his last breath after twelve minutes. The hospital were kind and thoughtful, making sure I had a private room, and asking if we wanted him baptised. Giving us time to hold him, being respectful, and not rushing us. Although I wanted to go home, I had to stay overnight for some medical treatment.

Coming home was hard, realising no-one would ever wear the tiny baby clothes laid out. The changing mat untouched. I stared at the Moses basket and wondered if it would ever not feel like a gaping wound. There was no mess, no crying, no night feeds. Breast milk being produced with no relief of feeding. Just stillness. And that stillness was deafening. The whispering of family downstairs, meaning well and trying to say the right things.

We had become parents again, and yet, felt invisible. There was no baby in the pram, no first steps, no first birthday, no first day of school, and no other firsts. But there was love. Fierce, aching, relentless love. Love that had nowhere to go but inward.

A feeling that nothing could possibly feel worse than this, and in my experience nothing ever did.

My first child, Ashley, was two when his brother was born. Life had to continue for him. He needed to know why I came home with no baby. He asked, and I answered as simply as I could. He still needed to go to his playgroups to have his routine, even when all I wanted to do was stay in bed and hide from the world. He needed me to carry on being his mum, armouring up every time I had to explain why I didn't have a baby with me.

This kind of grief doesn't announce itself. It shows up in quiet ways. A song I didn't expect to floor me. The moment you instinctively reach to check the time of a feed that will never come. It doesn't respond to timelines or tidy condolences. Torn between carrying on as normal, although nothing would feel normal again, and screaming inside.

A funeral to be planned, goodbyes to be said, decisions on who would be invited. Conversations about whether Ashley was too young to attend. I believed he wasn't. Stanley was his brother, and he had been prepared to be a big brother, and part of our healing was being able to say goodbye.

When we decided to try again, I wasn't replacing a child, I was learning how to mother one while still mourning another. It's a strange, sacred kind of duality, carrying hope and heartbreak at the same time. I held the flutter of new life in my womb while still aching for the baby I never got to cradle long enough.

People smiled when they heard the news, their joy genuine, their hope well meaning. But underneath their congratulations, I sometimes heard the unspoken assumption, maybe this will make things better. As if a new heartbeat could somehow mend the fracture left by the one that stopped. What they didn't see was that grief doesn't disappear just because joy returns. It doesn't get smaller when another child is born; it just shifts, reshapes, settles into new corners of your life. There were moments I wept over tiny socks, not because they were cute, but because I'd once folded a different pair, for a different child.

THE SILENCE THAT FOLLOWS

Moments I whispered to one baby while silently longing for the other. I didn't need to be told to be grateful; I was. But gratitude and grief can sit at the same table, and in my heart they did. Every day.

People might not know what to say. They may tiptoe around your grief, afraid to cause more pain. But the pain is already there. What helps isn't silence or avoidance, it's presence. Acknowledgement. A quiet, steady kindness that doesn't try to fix what cannot be fixed. Grief is not contagious, but people crossed the road so they didn't have to talk to me, and I could see the fear in their eyes and not knowing how to fix it! But you see, nothing needs fixing. All that needed to be said was as simple as, "I don't know what to say."

I wasn't broken. I was grieving. Having a baby-shaped hole that nothing could ever fill. I carry a story that is real, even if it is short. I have been told I should have got over it by now, and should I really be talking about him?

Some might measure life in years, milestones, photos on the fridge. But I know things are different. I know love can stretch across moments, across breaths. My baby existed. He mattered and he always will. For me, I have not got over it and never will; I live with it. Some days it's there like a soft hum, and other days it's right there sitting heavy on my chest before I even open my eyes.

And though the world may not see what I carry, I know the silence that follows is not empty; it's full – overflowing, in fact.

It holds memories. It holds meaning. It holds the shape of a life that changed mine and my family's forever.

I felt grief carving out a space within me. Not like a clean break or a sharp edge, but like water slowly wearing away rock. I didn't always notice it at first. The changes felt invisible. But then one day, I realised I was living inside a landscape that looks completely different than it did before the 17th of April, 1987.

After my son died, I found myself inhabiting that silence. Not just around me, but inside me. And yet, that stillness wasn't hollow. I was so afraid I wouldn't remember him and felt guilty if I laughed or briefly didn't think of him.

It was full of everything we never got to say, never got to do. It was full of dreams I had painted in my mind before he was born, the way he might have laughed, the way his hair might have curled at the ends, how his voice might have sounded calling my name.

Grief, I've learned, isn't just the pain of loss. I believe author Jamie Anderson said that grief is the presence of love with nowhere to go.

People often assume that when time passes, the pain should, too. That if you're smiling again or managing day-to-day tasks, the weight must have lifted. But grief doesn't work like that. It doesn't fade; it weaves itself into your every breath. It becomes the thread that binds you to what (and who) was lost.

I carry my son in the quietest places: in the pause before I answer how many children I have; in the way I notice the softness of other newborns; in the ache when birthdays come and go with no cake, no candles, just my thoughts and memories.

Through this, I found a quiet strength. Not the kind that looks brave on the outside, but the kind that shows up in whispered prayers, in getting out of bed on heavy days, in loving again without any guarantees. I learned how to mother through sorrow. How to make space for both joy and longing. And I discovered that honouring my son's memory didn't mean I couldn't fully love the child who came before and the one after him. It meant I had even more love to give. I was becoming something softer and stronger all at once. A mother shaped by absence, and also by the unshakable presence of love.

Grief has etched itself into my story, yes. But so has resilience, love, and the kind of strength that doesn't always roar. It whispers, *I am still here*. Still standing. Still loving. Still mothering in all the ways that matter most.

The silence isn't empty. It is a sacred space. A room within me that only he and I know how to enter.

And while the world may not see it, I do. Every single day.

If you're reading this and you've known a silence like this after a loss, after a goodbye that came too soon, then I hope you know that you are not alone in it. Your silence, too, holds meaning.

Grief has many forms, but at its heart is love undelivered, unspoken, or unfinished. And love like that doesn't disappear. It transforms. It teaches us how to listen to what can't be heard. To feel what can't be seen. To honour what can no longer be held.

So, if the world asks you to move on, let this be your permission to move differently. To move gently. To remember that the silence you carry is not a void. It is a vessel.

It holds your story. And it holds theirs, too.

I wrote this not as an expert or a guide, but as a mother still learning how to live with the shape of love that can no longer be held in my arms.

You don't have to explain your silence. You don't have to justify your sadness. You don't have to rush your healing.

May you find space in these words to breathe. To remember. To feel less alone in what you carry.

May the silence you hold always be honoured for what it truly is – love reshaped.

And though the silence remains, it no longer feels empty; it feels like a place where love echoes and memory lives on.

Dedication:

For Stanley

My second son

Born and died 17th April, 1987

You came quietly, but your presence was anything but small. You followed your big brother into this world, and though you couldn't stay, you deepened our family in ways words will never fully hold.

This chapter is for you, for the space you still fill, for the love you left behind, and for the way you continue to shape my heart, every single day.

Forever my son. Forever remembered. Forever loved.

Biography:

Kari is a Parent Empowerment Coach, International Best-Selling Author, and a sought-after speaker known for helping parents lead with calm, clarity, and confidence, even in the most challenging moments.

When emotions run high, words get tangled, or everything feels stuck, Kari doesn't offer surface fixes; she brings real change. With a grounded presence, practical tools, and zero judgment, she supports parents to navigate the tough parts of parenthood, manage conflict, and have difficult conversations that actually connect.

Her coaching, workshops, and resources are built around one core belief: empowered parenting starts with you. She helps you respond, not react, so you can feel confident in your parenting – even when it's hard – and see your family thrive.

You can connect with Kari here:

https://linktr.ee/kariann2309

How to Grieve a Guy in Three Ways

(Not A Romantic Comedy) By Emma Sails

"I keep my thoughts in little boxes, boxes underneath the bed, under the bed with your photograph, and the image is fading."
– The Bluetones, "Never Going Nowhere"

Content warning: This chapter mentions suicide and emotional abuse.

When I fell headfirst into the first long-term romantic relationship of my life, aged 17, I knew it would be a life-changing relationship. What I couldn't have known at the time is quite how life-changing, and in what context. In this chapter, I'm going to talk about my experience of grieving the same person three times.

Where it all began

We met in January 2002 and became friends a couple of months later. There was a group of us staying at my then boyfriend's house, and we travelled together for part of the journey... and oh how we laughed. Over the following couple of months, we spoke constantly, and I had never experienced anything like it; we could talk about anything, everything, and nothing, and it never got old. I felt completely seen and heard, and ok with being myself for the first time in my life. I had struggled a lot with social anxiety throughout my school life, and I was not in a good place mentally when we became close. To be fair, though, neither of us were.

In May 2002 we spent a weekend together at his house. He showed me where he grew up and told me about his childhood in a way that he'd never told it before. We laughed more than I ever had in my life. We started dating from that point, and it was a bit of a whirlwind; my life became entirely about him. So much of the early days of our relationship were filled with laughter, and we had given each other a purpose, which was absolutely everything to me.

We moved in together just after I turned 18. I moved across the country, and we got a flat together. It was everything I'd ever wanted, and I was so incredibly happy.

The break-up

When you realise that your fairytale ending wasn't quite what you'd thought it would be, there is a grieving process to go through... so this was the first time I grieved this person. I grieved the connection we'd had and the life I had thought we would have together.

Initially, I was absolutely determined that we could make things work out, so in February 2006 the purchase of our house went through. The house, in my mind, was going to save our relationship by giving us space to breathe and by moving us forward. I was, of course, completely in denial that the relationship was over and was clutching at any straws I could find. I'd been feeling increasingly claustrophobic living in a one-bedroomed flat together, and I'd all but stopped socialising. We travelled to work together each day, and he was in the same room as me for the majority of the time at home. So, in a three-bedroomed house it was definitely going to be better, right? No, it wasn't better.

Instead of being in the same room constantly, we barely saw each other at home. I felt utterly alone, and I was absolutely heartbroken about where I'd found myself. The connection we'd had was gone, but I felt trapped. We still spent all our time together outside of the house, and to the outside world we seemed like the perfect couple, completely wrapped up in our own lives and in each other.

But my confidence was absolutely on the floor, I was severely depressed and anxious, and felt disgusted by my physical appearance. I had found myself in a massive financial hole after taking on joint debt in solely my name, and I didn't have a clue what to do about it.

In May 2006, three months after buying a house together, I tried to end that relationship for the first time. I'd told a few people over the few days before, so that I'd have some support from my friends, and almost everyone was absolutely floored by the decision. Of course, that made it a lot harder. *(Tip for you – if someone says they're ending their relationship, the only right thing to do is to be 100% supportive. You don't know what they've gone through to get there!)* And then, when I did have that conversation, it did not go down well with him at all. I was ruining his life, I'd talked him into buying a house, I'd trapped him in this situation and was then abandoning him, I was being incredibly selfish, he couldn't function without me, it was a huge mistake, and we would both end up miserable and alone, and ultimately, he was going to kill himself.

We talked it all through and I decided to stay. We were going to go out more, to do pub quizzes, go on day trips, and socialise with our friends. It was going to be better; things were going to change. They did not change.

Three months later, I desperately needed a way out of the relationship, and I couldn't see how to do that without being responsible for ruining both of our lives. But I also couldn't see a future for my life inside that relationship. I felt trapped and completely alone.

So, I cheated on him. I did the worst thing I could conceivably think of doing… whilst at the same time giving myself just the smallest bit of confidence that, actually, I might walk away and not end up miserable and alone. In my mind at the time, I absolutely would not cheat on someone I loved. So that was also a way to prove to myself that I was no longer in love with this person.

After cheating, I knew I really needed to leave, but I couldn't see how I could end the relationship without being talked back into staying yet again. And I didn't know what he would do on finding out I'd cheated. One morning, I did our usual commute to work with him, and then I went home and packed a bag and left. I texted him to say I wasn't coming back, and that I needed to give us both a couple of days to process things before we could have a conversation in person.

I was absolutely torn up by the way I had done things. I felt like I was completely responsible for ruining both of our lives and destroying the thing I had wanted more than anything a few short years before. I felt selfish and cowardly for years afterwards, but at the same time I couldn't see any other way that I could have left.

One thing that did really help me at the time was music. I was listening to The Bluetones' song I quoted above on repeat, and the repetition of "I don't love you anymore" in the lyrics helped massively. I knew for sure that staying with someone that you don't love anymore isn't fair, and yes, I regretted the way I had done things, but in my eyes at the time there was no other way.

In the months following this, he moved on and made sure I knew that he had "levelled up". I ended up living in a dingy flat riddled with mice and fleas, living above a woman who used to hammer the floorboards with a broom handle if she heard me moving about after 6pm. But I was free and able to start building my life back up again.

The six to nine months after ending that relationship were the hardest of my life so far, and the enormous amount of grief, processing, and questioning that happened in that time have massively shaped my future. But there was no point when I considered going back.

Trusting my instinct to leave, finding a way to do that, and staying away, is one of the things I'm now most grateful to myself for.

The suicide

Fast forward to early 2014, and my ex and I were loosely back in touch. There'd been a few instances over the years where we'd spoken or met up, for various reasons, and our friendship was fine. Just after his 30th birthday, he was going through a rough time. Back then I was running an accountancy business, and I helped him create a plan for building a business going forward and setting up self-employment for himself. We had an exceptionally long phone call in mid-May, for around three hours, chatting about good memories that we had and talking about his plans for the future. It was a really positive phone call, and I came away from it feeling like I'd helped him work through some of the issues he'd been having, and that he could start looking towards the future.

One night in June, at 10pm, I received an email from him that I will never forget.

"IMPORTANT! Read me immediately" was the subject. The content said that the email had been sent on a timer, that he had killed himself, and that we were to send an ambulance to his address to pick him up. I later found out that it had been sent to two people – the other being one of my now best friends – because we were the most likely to check our emails in a timely manner (the phrase 'in a timely manner' still makes me shudder). That night, and the following few days, were absolute hell... but he survived. I'd never imagined I'd see anyone so very angry at waking up as he was that day, but he survived.

He was discharged and went home within a few days, I kept checking in on him via message over the coming weeks: daily at first, and then every few days. And he was always "getting there". He had various medical issues that were related to the attempt, but he was on the road to recovery.

One Sunday in mid-August, I received a phone call from the same friend who had been involved in June. He'd tried suicide again, but this time he had been successful. You know when everything passes in front of your eyes and you're not quite sure what is going on at all? That. Everything went hazy. How could this have happened? I knew he'd been able to convince the hospital that he was doing well, but I was appalled at myself for believing his tales of getting there.

Initially, there was so much blame. I had known him longest, so I should have seen through it and been able to support him more. He had always said that his intention was to die by suicide, and he had in fact tried not long after we initially got together. But I'd saved him then, and again when he had involved me in June 2014, which had somehow made me believe I could keep saving him.

The next few days were a blur, mainly spent trying to support my friend who had been the one to find him, and to try and make some sense of what had happened. There were a lot of issues around finding his next of kin, because as far as everyone involved in his current life was concerned, he had no living family. And I wasn't close enough anymore to know any different. Once the police found out that his family were still very much alive, though, my place in this became clear. I was the only person who could be the link between his new life and his old, and the only person who knew his family.

He had, of course, known that I would step in and do exactly what he needed me to do. I helped to arrange the funeral, to communicate between friends and family, to make introductions that needed making, and to sort possessions that his family were still storing. This was my ex-partner from eight years before, yet here I was helping to arrange everything and behaving like we were still very close and nothing had changed.

I remember speaking to the humanist minister who was trying to build a picture of his life for the service, and talking about our relationship through the rose-tinted spectacles that grief so often provides. I explained how we'd saved each other in our teens and had such a deep understanding of each other. And I told how it had often been said to me that we'd met at the wrong time in our lives for it to work, but that we were so well matched.

It was an exceptionally confusing time and brought back a lot of memories that I'd squashed down. I hadn't been very close to him for almost eight years, so I felt out of place being involved. But at the same time, feeling like I had to provide that connection, I was being pulled back into the past. I hadn't experienced a similar connection with anyone else since we were together, so at times it was somehow like mourning a current relationship.

Suicide is an absolutely horrible thing to deal with for the family and friends of that person, and its impact spreads far beyond anything that could be conceived beforehand. People he had met or spoken to years ago in passing were reaching out, sending messages of sympathy, and donating to the fundraiser we had set up for him.

Personally, I had struggled with suicidal ideation twice in my life before experiencing suicide from this perspective... and this made me absolutely determined that I would never put the people around me through that. A few years later, I struggled massively with it whilst pregnant, and a big part of what helped me through was knowing the impact it would have on those around me. Living for other people is not something to do for a whole lifetime, but in the short term it has really helped me to have the knowledge of the impact it could have if I wasn't here.

The realisation

Fast forward to October 2021, and I had a failed marriage behind me, was a single parent, and was just starting to date again. When I started my work as a coach, I quickly realised that there was a lot from my life that needed unpicking, so I'd been in therapy for quite some time by then. The relationship I'd been in from ages 17-21 was something that had impacted every area of my life since, but it had 'just' been a toxic relationship, right?

I met my current partner through a dating app, and when we first started messaging, time just disappeared. We could talk about anything, everything, and nothing, and it never got old. Our first date was a few drinks in his local. We spent most of the date talking about such random things that we were getting funny looks from the other people in the pub, and oh how we laughed... I hadn't laughed that way with a potential romantic partner in years, not since... oh.

I was absolutely terrified of history repeating itself from the very start.

As I got to know my partner more, and we experienced more together, there were additional triggers. There were quite a few things that my current partner and my ex had in common, and lots of things that we experienced together that would have had very different outcomes in my past life. Outfits I wore that wouldn't have been allowed ("you can't wear that, it makes you look like a wh*re"), conversations I had and things I did with friends that we could have potentially done together ("how dare you go and see that film without telling me; we should have gone together, and now there are consequences"), and so on.

I spent a lot of time bracing myself for what was to come, and there was a lot to work through with my new partner. But he spent a lot of time reassuring me that he was not the same as my ex and would never react in that way. I felt awful for making the connection and for needing the reassurance. It felt like I was being offensive to my partner to even make that association, but it was so far out of my control and just kept happening.

In late 2023, we set the wheels in motion to buy a house together and started going to view properties. When I set foot in the second house we viewed, it was as though my brain melted. I managed to get through the viewing and hold my face, but I have no idea how; it was like I was watching a car crash unfurl. I got in the car afterwards and drove home sobbing, convinced that if we proceeded with the house purchase, everything was going to go disastrously wrong. My partner had absolutely loved the house, and logistically I could understand why; it was perfect for us from the outside, and I had been able to imagine us living there whilst looking round. But... I had been able to imagine us living there and everything falling apart. I felt such an enormous sense of foreboding, and it sent me into a complete spiral.

I took my reaction to my next therapy session and asked what I could do to figure out what had happened, and what I should do next. After a brief conversation, I was asked the question: "The relationship you ended in 2006, was that an abusive relationship?" My immediate answer was "of course not", but then we explored it, and slowly I started to see everything from a new perspective that I hadn't previously considered. I felt sick; in fact, I very nearly was sick.

For years I had carried so much guilt for the period surrounding our break-up, but the simple reframe of "what kind of relationship requires you to leave in secret?" was absolutely mind-blowing. It had been an emotionally abusive relationship. I had been emotionally abused.

This realisation all happened a couple of weeks before my now deceased ex's 40th birthday, and on that day, I was a mess. I had spent years marking it as a way to remember him. I would routinely go out and buy his favourite drink and chocolate bar and take a moment to reflect. But now I was incensed that I had spent so many years and so much energy devoted to remembering this person who had emotionally abused me.

Initially, there was a lot of anger – both at him and at myself. I'd often ask myself how I could have been so stupid as not to realise. And even in writing the first part of this chapter and telling the story exactly how I'd have told it back in 2006, how did I not realise? While you're in that, though, while someone is constantly blaming you for everything that goes wrong and insisting that you're the problem, it is so difficult to see that actually you're not.

In my mind, I had always justified the way that relationship had been because of my ex's mental health; he was very insecure, needed a lot of reassurance, and to feel in control.

Looking back now, after having put the work in to process everything that happened, I can see that it doesn't really matter what was going on for him; that doesn't mean it didn't happen; and it doesn't mean my experience isn't valid. Just because someone is troubled, it doesn't give them an excuse to be controlling, manipulative, and cruel. Just because someone is troubled, it doesn't mean that it was ok for me to be demeaned, controlled, isolated, and essentially squashed.

Once I finally knew all this, I had to go through and reassess my perspective on everything that had happened over the last 18 years. And I had to process the fact I had dropped everything ten years earlier to ensure that my abuser had the best final farewell that he could have had. I reflected on the stories I'd told the humanist minister of how we'd saved each other and how it had often been said to me that we'd just met each other at the wrong time. Looking at the period of mourning through a different lens meant I had to grieve both the lost relationship and the loss of the person all over again... coupled with new loss – the loss of autonomy I realised I'd had while we lived together, and the loss of confidence and self-respect that had impacted years of my life.

Grief and trauma are so very entangled, and it is impossible at times to separate them. It is so important to acknowledge, though, that they can both be worked through, and you don't have to be a victim forever. Therapy has helped me enormously; a year ago, the thought of sitting here writing about this would have been torture. And whilst it is still difficult, I have made peace with what has happened, and it no longer impacts my life every day, or in fact often at all.

In summary

I've spent a lot of time working through this relationship and the various kinds of grief it has caused, and now there's no way I would go back and change it. To say that everything happens for a reason is a gross over-simplification, but I know that I definitely would not be where I am now without these experiences.

Here I want to list a few of the things I've learned through my experiences that will hopefully be helpful to those reading:

1. Everything that you experience is valid, and trusting your instincts is absolutely vital. If you are struggling in a relationship and things aren't feeling right, there is a good chance that they're *not* right. Remember that you deserve to be happy and to feel loved; sometimes things can be worked through, and sometimes it's ok (and it's always possible) to walk away.

2. There are no 'shoulds' or 'shouldn'ts' when it comes to grief, because it is unique to every person. Whatever you are feeling when experiencing a loss, it's completely ok for you to move forward in your own way. Shortly after my dad died in 2015, someone at work said to me that I'd seemed to care a lot more when my ex-partner had died than I did about Dad. Obviously, that was very hurtful, but it was based around her experience of losing her parents young, rather than about my experience. My experience of losing my dad *was* awful, but it wasn't traumatic.

3. Beating yourself up for "letting things happen" isn't going to help anyone. Until you realise a situation is toxic or causing trauma, you are unlikely to realise you need to get out of it.

Once you realise, though, you have a choice to make – it's time to make a change.

4. It is always, always, worth doing the work, processing, and letting yourself move on... and it is completely OK to move on.

I am sitting here today, about to submit my chapter to this book, and it is the first anniversary of moving into the house I bought with my partner (now fiancé). If I could say one thing to that 21-year-old me who was leaving an abusive relationship and dreading what the future would bring, it would be this:

One day you will wake up in a house that you adore, next to a man that is everything that you could ever want, raising a child who is happy and healthy, and you will feel supported, encouraged, appreciated, and loved for being just as you are. It isn't going to be easy... but you will get there.

Dedication:

To Kate, my amazing therapist, for being patient and supportive, and for helping me process all of the things. And to Ste, who has shown me just how good things can be.

Biography:

Emma Sails is an ICF-accredited life coach who has done a significant amount of neurodivergent specific training. She works as a coach and mentor with neurodivergent adults and parents of neurodivergent children, to help them understand and accept how neurodivergence impacts their lives, and what they can do to stop it from holding them back.

When Emma found out about her own neurodivergence aged 35, everything changed for her. She had just come through a battle with post-natal depression and ended her marriage, and she was on a mission to figure out what she wanted in life and how to be the best role model for her son.

Diagnosis of ADHD and autism gave her an answer to a lot of the struggles she'd faced throughout her life, and she set out to spread awareness and help others on the same journey. Emma's ultimate goal is to ensure that future generations of neurodivergent children don't have to go through the same trials growing up as her generation did.

You can connect with Emma here:
https://linktr.ee/EmmaSailsCoaching

Grace in Grief

Grace, Growth, Glory – How to Manage the Unmanageable with Hope, Love and a Bit of Joy By Rebecca Williams Dinsdale

"Love so amazing, so divine,
Demands my soul, my life, my all."
– I. Watts

Introduction...

I took my Mother's funeral. That's not an easy sentence to write. It was a much harder thing to do. I didn't just read a poem, give a eulogy or take part, I did it all. The whole sad show was on my shoulders. It was such a cold day in my childhood Church where everyone looked lost and mournful. Going up the aisle was the loneliest walk in the world even though I had great love around me. My nose wouldn't stop running, but I didn't cry or gasp. God held me up. We even had smiles and kind laughs, a lot of nods and good singing. We had a lot.

When we got to the crematorium, I knew it would be demanding but the sight of our friend clinging to the door with her walker and oxygen machine was humbling. She was near the end of life herself and yet forced her failing body to stand at our side. My Mother adored her. Ironically, our friend then asked me to plan and conduct her funeral, which was one of the most profound days of my life.

I had to take my Mother's funeral. My love for her was too great to let her go with anyone else. Sometimes when I tell people that I did this, they are shocked and look at me for a moment with incredulity. The best of souls offer me a look of immense empathy and wonder how on earth it was possible. The less-than-best offer comments that I won't waste words on here, but I know what it took because she was mine and I was hers.

The real difficulty was not the actual day of the funeral because her suffering was over by then, we only had to deal with our own which was much more manageable than seeing her tortured. Our real grief was witnessing the excruciating 14 years of her gradual destruction with varying levels of medical assistance and having to battle multiple systems for sometimes inadequate care.

I am proud of our battles for her, but we should never have had to have them, they made everything unnecessarily difficult. We met arrogance, ignorance and a stalling bureaucracy repeatedly, which was exhausting and demoralising. We consoled ourselves in the angelic help that emerged from unlikely sources and honourable people who did their jobs with grace and gusto. She had already endured so much illness and lack of normal life before this hit her. It really wasn't fair.

I have raged silently when seeing the easy lives of others and I pleaded that my precious parents could have just an inch of it or at least less suffering. Living with the fear of what horror might befall them next leaves you untrusting of life. All my work has been, and continues to be, about helping others offset these fears with wise courage and coping strategies. The example has been set for me by my Father whose resourcefulness and good temper have been extraordinary. How my Mother was blessed to find him.

I don't want to be negative, embittered or fearful, so I work extra hard to be cheerful and resourceful. So how did we get here?

As an only child, born on my Mother's birthday, I was always in a unique position. Today, with a magnificent Father and beautiful Husband, I have gifts beyond measure. My Mother, Father and I have been chased by so much illness which has taught us to cherish normal life with a voracity that surprises many. After decades of restriction, reduction and degeneration; we know an alarming amount about struggle. I use the word 'struggle' mindfully as my brave Father says, "We are not to think of ourselves as suffering but working to find a way through." We are good workers. We are good prayers. We are good at struggle and sadly, well-versed with suffering. We are very good at counting our blessings and knowing that so many people are in a worse position.

Between us, we have had complex chronic illness, severe M.E., just about every problem with food, joint problems, a failing pancreas, and for my Mother, early onset dementia with psychosis and epilepsy thrown in just to make life more complex. Yet I hope and pray that we are not defined by these conditions, even though they have dominated our lives for so long. I just want to be normal; where health is taken for granted and life can go on; plans can be made and met; pals can be partied with and places discovered. Maybe just being able to function, breathe, eat and feel comfortable would be marvellous; please never,

ever, take for granted the ability to get yourself to the bathroom, tolerate enough food and just be at ease.

So that's the basics of the setup. We did everything right and it all went horribly wrong. We worked hard and behaved well – we held up our end of the social contract, but it wasn't enough. Yet somehow, I find myself talking to you now, still here, wanting to pass on some help and hope. I want to be your friend. I want to give you a hug and tell you that you're brave and you've done well for getting this far. I want to reassure you that even though this is horrid, you are still you and still have much ahead of you. Your wounds will heal a bit, reopen and then mend a bit more and your life ahead can be filled with more loving people and happy times. You just need to hold on long enough to get there – and the holding on part might be a lot longer than anyone else will ever realise. So, get good at holding on.

Are you wondering what it was like for me to take the funeral of my loved one? I wish you could know deeply about the love part and never need to know about the funeral part. But the reality is that most people will have to deal with grief and sorting out a service at some point in their lives. The later you have to deal with it, the more fortunate you have been.

My experience as a Christian Celebrant...

As a Christian Celebrant, I have taken about a thousand loving funeral services. Because I had experienced such illness at a young age, I understood the grief that my clients were facing much later in life. That was the loving purpose that emerged from all that adversity. That prolonged level of difficulty needed to be used for a good purpose. Every single family in my care became my family for those most intense days and weeks around a bereavement. I tried my best to look after them as if they were mine because they were. Many have remained among my closest friends.

Now here is the insightful part – taking services for them was just as hard as looking after my Mother. She would have been the first to send me out to take care of them and acknowledge that somehow there is a range of losses in life. Celebrating the life of a 99-year-old who has lived a healthy, productive and joyous life is a privilege. It is not a tragedy that they had to leave, it is a reality of life. The tragedies are too many to mention but once you've taken funerals for tiny babies, little children, teenagers, young parents and victims of accidents, attacks, abuse and suicide, as well as misdiagnosis and medical negligence – you realise just what torturous pain means. I have seen people so hurt by injustice that I feared they would never recover. I have seen the bravest and best of humanity in every possible way show me just what the human soul can endure and keep loving. It's the love that does it. The love that won't let go, keeps trying and offers comfort to those in similar circumstances – that is the real power within all of us.

I have held people who collapsed into my embrace unable to bear their loss and I have come away with the deepest feeling that, after seeing their valour, I would never complain about anything else ever again. I hold onto that reminder when I start to fuss about inconsequential things because a lot of life's challenges are more inconsequential than we think.

- Please know that you can feel terrible for a long time, yet hope can return.

- Please believe that you can suffer injustices and goodness can still prevail.

- Please know that you are more valuable to our world because of your sufferings as they have stretched you, so your empathy is greater.

Anticipatory grief...

There is a form of grief that few speak about, that of anticipatory loss. It involves knowing what is coming. It can involve a series of slow and sad losses where functioning decreases and dependency increases. The feeling that life is draining away whilst we are desperately trying to save someone is immensely hard to bear... but bear it we must.

I wish I could tell you that it won't be as bad as you fear. But I can't. What I can tell you, from brutal and extensive experience, is that you will cope with more than you could ever imagine. Your whole life is an apprenticeship for this purpose. This might just be your most important work. To be at the side of a loved one is a mighty privilege and their trust in your presence is one of the greatest gifts. However, privileges and gifts can be heavy blessings so be prepared to be tested, stretched and challenged in unimaginable ways. But you can cope. Remember that. You have coped, you are coping and you will cope. It may not be glamorous or easy, but it is possible. And get as much help as possible from professionals, charities, local support groups and pals.

The other part of anticipatory grief is that it happens not just with death. It delivers itself with ongoing illness – the losses that happen incrementally and violently – the loss of opportunities, expectations and assumptions of what your life might have been. Education reduced or shortened, employment and careers unmanaged, holidays impossible, gentle hobbies too much and even pottering about with just enough energy to cope – they can all be lost. There is hurt in those rejections. There is immense stress from worrying about income, bills, benefits and terrible headlines in newspapers that belittle your imposed and unwanted plight. When you're flying, nobody tells you what it feels like to be called, "unemployable" or that you should, "try a bit harder and try this remedy" and all would be well.

Perhaps the greatest indignity of it all might be dealing with ignorance from those who ought to know better or those paid to offer care; medics who dismiss you or make things worse, admin staff who can't get important things right and medicine shortages that make everything worse. These are grievous things indeed.

My only counter to them would be the love that can be witnessed. The porter who pushes you along a bumpy corridor with sensitivity, the doctor who sends a message to find out if you got your meds, the pal who sends a kind post to cheer you and the people who keep visiting. They are the treasures of the time and the ones to emulate.

I aspire and endeavour to be one of those helpful people wherever I can. My only advice to you would be, if in doubt, then try! Try to visit, send something or just ask what they need. Do it. Don't let the phrase, "I don't want to intrude," delay you.

Then there is the unspoken grace that must be cherished, when people are gracious and pop out of the woodwork to help. The kind of people you wouldn't expect to pop out and they suddenly show themselves as true champions. They are the ones who are pleased for your tiny pieces of progress or moments of relief.

Of course, some people stay firmly in the woodwork and avoid you at all costs. Forget about them, the wood needs them more than you. If they can't cope, then you don't need them. Let them go with love and relief.

Also, know that people will be insensitive even when they are trying their very best, so extend more grace to them. There is a way to cope with your ongoing grief and the ongoing glory in the lives of others. Just be pleased for them.

One of the greatest assets of any character, especially a war-weary one, is to be glad for the goodness that happens around you. Learning to be super gracious and super resilient is not an easy syllabus but it is a vital one if you're to survive almost intact. I am now an expert at pulling my face into sheer delight every time I hear of someone's triumph because even though I have been desperate for their triumphs I know they deserve them and not any kind of misery or sadness. Again, I return to the fact that even with my shabby lot, a lot of people will think that I am very fortunate. I am.

Practicalities...

From a practical perspective, I would urge you to think about your life today: how you live it daily. What you think, say and do matters. It matters that you protect your sleep, nutrition, hydration and happiness. It matters that you look after yourself and others at work, play and home. It matters that you bring your creativity and contributions to your community. They need you.

Your spirituality and faith ought to be the foundations of your life and if you can't find that yet, then volunteer, donate or give of yourself to start the journey to fulfil your potential. Don't be ashamed to wander in silence, to be still or to develop gratitude for the tiny treasures in life. Pray, even if you don't believe! Just try. Let go of self-recrimination and judgemental attitudes and build boundaries that bless everyone. Remember your self-worth and make whatever you do, your mission to leave a loving mark on this world. Find good friends and be one.

Laugh as much as you can and give your time to good souls. Deal with your difficulties with as much dignity and backbone as you can muster. Don't allow guilt, resentment, embitterment or negativity find a home in you. Wash them off every time you're well enough to have a shower.

Make a life list, not a bucket one. What do you want people to say about you at your funeral? Is it that you were reliable, kind and fun? These are the values that form our intentions that go on to shape our relationships and lives. Find work that allows you to offer your talents in service and manage your finances with ethical choices and long-term wisdom.

If you need any kind of help, advice or support then please seek it. Sort out a Will and Power of Attorney and plan the kind of life you would like at the end and the levels of intervention needed. The earlier you accept help, the less you might need. Sometimes a bit of help at home, or a respite stay at a care home or hospice, might turn out to be utterly loving. If you have choices, then appreciate them and think about the implications for your loved ones.

Declutter! Write letters to your precious people declaring how proud you are of them. If you're able to think about what you would like in terms of funeral service, write it down and have a calm chat about it with them. Maybe even plan the contents of the service and details of the music and ceremony you would like, or if you would prefer not to have a service or do something else entirely.

Counselling and coaching...

I now spend my working life as a counsellor and life coach. One of the foundations of my work is to help clients help themselves – so please don't smoke, avoid alcohol, be careful with caffeine and ditch sugary drinks. I detest booze and pop because I've seen what it does to the metabolic system. What we consume has a huge impact on the quality and quantity of our lives. Trust me. Health and unity matter more than you can ever realise. Before every decision ask yourself, "Is this wise?"

Here is the deepest truth of life – death is coming for us all, so we need to think about it with a measured approach. I've written five books on courage, joy and hope and after giving over a thousand eulogies, the most profound were for the people who had loved joyously and made the most of their potential. They had been wise, generous and proactive in life, navigating their challenges with a resolute approach and enduring the unexpected hits in life with self-possession.

Grief in the latter stages of life...

Grief in the latter stages needs to be managed with a different set of coping strategies than in the early days. The early days can be like an indeterminate prison sentence of hard labour. They are to be endured and will be demanding until there might be the possibility of parole for getting this far. Parole might only mean a minuscule respite, but anything is better than relentless pain. Our parole officers are our helpers, counsellors, ministers and kind souls who offer what they can. Sometimes we are our own and sometimes we are those roles for others. Even in the depths of despair, we can still offer help to others.

When we allow ourselves to feel the shots of pain, we honour the love that has been bestowed on us. There will always be a sharp intake of breath for me on Mothering Sunday and every time I see a pregnancy. I could think that my Mother was taken far too soon in a tragic and torturous decline, which is true, yet I can also think that I was so blessed to have her for the time that was allocated. Every newborn I hold, I still do not want to give back. When I was little, I heard a news report about a baby being abandoned in a telephone box and to this day, every time I see a phone box, I just check to see if I am to come to the rescue. It is ridiculous but true and when someone troops into Church with their little ones it makes me sob inside that we won't have that gift and that I couldn't deliver it for my precious ones. Yet our friends are our family, so we do our best to be family to them.

BUT, I must find a place within myself to allow those dualities to exist whilst knowing that every child I encounter might leave my company feeling treasured. To hold myself to account, I remember the worst days of utterly tragic losses and that there are a thousand people who would swap with me and my lot in life. My conclusion that seems endlessly helpful is to know that I am very blessed in many areas of life, in the ones that truly matter to me – the quality of my Grandparents, Parents and Partner. We have faced multiple challenges that have been neither balanced nor fair. One does not negate the other, they just need to be managed with grace.

Grief of disappointing behaviour...

Finally, the grief of disappointing behaviour is perhaps one of the hardest to manage. We can wish that someone didn't make things worse, act out their selfishness and be proactively nasty, or we can hold a wise boundary, defend what is worthy and let the rest go. Life will be what it will be. They are none of our business now.

I could write an entire book on the antics that I have witnessed in planning and delivering funeral services. There have been petty arguments that blow up worlds, with the astonishing dramas and the hysteria produced usually by those who have done the least to help. Epic displays of emotion can be outward performances whilst the depth of tragic heartbreak rarely has spare energy to squander. They don't make a hard situation hellish for everyone else.

People tend to behave better when in Church but when you get to the crem or the wake, that's when it can kick off! So here is my counter to that – one of the most useful things that I said in the crem for my Mother was this, "Sometimes you just can't keep going if you're in hell, but if you're lucky there will be someone to pull you through." Be the person who holds on to the lost souls and allow yourself to be helped. Try and be resourceful and polite, muster what cheerfulness you can and hold on. Don't make things worse with bad behaviour. It helps no one.

My Mother...

I took my Mother's funeral because it was the right thing to do. I loved her. She loved me. God formed us both to know that we are fearfully and wonderfully made – however shabby and raggy we are in this life. Oh, and I want you to know that my Mummy was called Marion. She was ultra-loyal, clever, funny and faithful. Her ability to see the needs of the lost lamb showed a sensitivity that was astounding. Generosity, impulsivity and a loving wisdom shone from her. As a teacher and protector of little souls, she played her piano in school halls and gave them as much protection and empowerment as possible.

I met many of her former pupils who went on to be my friends and clients. The serendipity of this astonished me and they all said that my Mummy was pretty and kind. They saw what we saw – just from a little person's perspective. With that level of devotion, you would want to speak of her, you would want to take her funeral. It was a service of loving appreciation.

To conclude...

So, how do we bring this together? I wanted to write something that would help you. I really hope it has been of use. My empirical maxim is always, "The way to live well, is to love well." To be able to love well after loss needs us to be able to say and live out:

"Thank you for loving me so well, I will love you eternally

I will take all the blessings and lessons of your life

to keep your light shining."

Therefore, my friend, I will leave you with this most powerful hope. If you're reading this book with a broken soul, please know this – I am sure that your loved one is in Heaven now and will be rejoicing in you. Rejoice in the fact that you were privileged to belong to each other and go forward and live as they would wish you to do. Be more yourself, be more loving, more joyous, braver, wiser and stronger for their care. Love as vibrantly as you can for as long as you can. Wrap the pain with grace.

Be the love. I know you will do well, my friend. And maybe, just maybe, my little Mummy will be taking care of your loved one whilst they are watching over us all. I hope so. I pray so. Amen.

Dedication:

To Ivy, Nigel, Marion, and Kevin – thank you for loving me so well. I will love you eternally.

Biography:

Rebecca Williams Dinsdale PhD is the Award-Winning Lifejoy Coach, Author of 5 Transformational Books, Speaker & Guide for Burnout Recovery.

With decades of experience in health, academia and heart-led coaching, she empowers people to become braver, wiser and more joyous – no matter their starting point.

She has helped countless individuals rediscover their spark, reclaim their peace, and create a life aligned with purpose and joy. Her five published books offer uplifting and practical guidance to help you find your own light, even on the darkest days.

Having worked as a Christian Celebrant, she has conducted more than a thousand loving funeral services which, alongside speaking, writing and coaching, has created her unique understanding about love, loss and loyalty.

After decades of intense struggle with health, Rebecca developed her Lifejoy philosophy to use that enduring adversity to a loving purpose. Lifejoy stands for Love, Integrity, Fortitude, Energy, Joy, Order and You.

Rebecca is the patron of the mental health charity, Headlight, which she describes as an island of sanity in a world of chaos.

Sunflowers are the emblem of her Lifejoy work, as they seek the light and when the storms come, they hold one another together.

You can connect with Rebecca here:
https://linkt.ree.DrRebecca

Other Collaborative Projects

By Cassie Swift

Hold on to Hope

Hold on to Hope brings together 19 amazing women who are sharing their stories to overcoming challenges they have faced. This book aims to share that, by holding on to hope, you will be able to overcome any situation you are faced with! The women in this book have found their healing and peace by sharing their stories – one day this could be you too.

You can order your copy here:

Also available at Blackwell's and Barnes & Noble

What I Wish I Had Heard

What I Wish I Had Heard: Stories From Our Inner Child, brings together ten incredible and inspirational women in a powerful and heartfelt collaboration where they share stories from their inner child. They have had to dig deep to connect with the younger versions of themselves to present you their stories about feelings of worth, bullying, abuse, and so many more. Not only has this brought them healing and peace, but we hope that it will introduce you to just how powerful the concept of the inner child is and may even start you on your own healing journey.

The chapters share stories of self discovery and deep connection as well as activities the authors themselves have used to aid their healing. With the added bonus of audio links, it also means it is accessible for everyone to benefit from.

Remember, you are not alone or broken, healing is open to everyone including YOU!

You can order your copy here:

Also available at Blackwell's and Barnes & Noble

Navigating Anxiety with Children & Teens

Navigating Anxiety with Children & Teens shares advice, strategies and real life examples from a collaboration of 13 experts in their field. It focuses on ways to navigate different forms of anxiety, from how we frame the term 'anxiety', to dealing with terminal illness, to the very real mum guilt. The aim is to aid you in supporting our younger generation as well as reminding you that you are not alone - there are many people available to help you on this journey.

The chapters share real life stories and activities on dealing with the many different forms of anxiety our young people face. With the added bonus of audio links, it also means it is accessible for everyone to benefit from. If you are struggling to navigate anxiety then this book is a must read for you.

You can order your copy here:

Also available at Blackwell's and Barnes & Noble

Children's Mental Health Matters

Children's Mental Health Matters: shares advice, strategies, and real-life examples from a collaboration of 14 experts in their field. Covering many areas from high-conflict divorce, migration, emotional regulation, to self-harm and seeing things from a dad's perspective, the book aims to help support our younger generation in navigating the many challenges they now face in modern society,
as well as reminding you that you are not alone.

The authors share real-life stories, examples, activities, and practical advice on dealing with many different aspects of life that affect our young people's mental health. The added bonus of audio links
means it is accessible for everyone.

With thanks to the authors: Cassie Swift, Sara Bowater, Sarah Burnett, Duncan Casburn, Fleur Conway, Amy Dalwood-Fairbanks, Lucy

Fenwick, AJ Gajjar, Lucy Harper, Keri Hartwright, Laura Linklater, Emily Nuttall, Jules Reynolds and Emma Sails.

You can order your copy here:

Also available at Blackwell's and Barnes & Noble